UNLEASH WEALTH WITH MUTUAL FUNDS

Unlock Your Wealth by Mastering Mutual Funds for A Wealthier Tomorrow!

JAYESH CHOPADE

ISBN: 979-88-73383-95-5

CONTENTS

PREFACE

Dear Readers,

Welcome to the exciting world of wealth creation through mutual funds! I am delighted to share with you the insights, strategies, and possibilities that come with navigating the dynamic landscape of mutual fund investments.

As we embark on this journey together, I want to express my heartfelt gratitude. This book has been a labor of love, fueled by a passion for financial empowerment and a deep belief in the transformative potential of mutual funds.

The idea for this book sprouted from countless conversations with individuals seeking to understand how to make their money work for them. In today's fast-paced world, where financial decisions are increasingly complex, I felt a calling to demystify the realm of mutual funds and empower readers with the knowledge to unleash their wealth potential.

In these pages, you will discover not just the mechanics of mutual fund investments but also the art of wealth creation. We'll explore the diverse range of mutual fund options, dissect investment strategies, and unravel the secrets to making informed financial decisions.

Throughout my journey of exploring and investing in mutual funds, I've encountered challenges and celebrated victories. It's these experiences that have shaped the content of this book. I want you to feel the excitement that comes with unleashing the wealth-building power of mutual funds, but I also want to equip you with the wisdom to navigate the inevitable twists and turns of the financial landscape.

This book is not just a guide; it's a companion on your wealth creation journey. Whether you are a seasoned investor or someone taking the first steps into the world of mutual funds, I've crafted these pages to offer valuable insights, practical tips, and a roadmap to financial success.

As you immerse yourself in the following chapters, remember that wealth creation is not a one-size-fits-all endeavor. Each of you brings a unique financial footprint, and it's my sincere hope that this book serves as a tailored guide to unleashing your wealth potential.

Thank you for entrusting me with a part of your financial education. Let's embark on this journey together and unleash the wealth that mutual funds have to offer.

Wishing you prosperity and financial fulfillment,

Jayesh Chopade

INTRODUCTION

Last month when I met my friend, I asked him whether he had started investing in mutual funds, but his answer was NO. So, I asked him the reason and he gave me a few like it is not my cup of tea, it's for experts, it needs lots of money to invest in mutual funds, and I need to wait for the right time to invest in Mutual Funds, investing in mutual funds is a complex task.

If you are also thinking about these reasons, let me tell you that I call them MUTUAL FUND MYTHS.

Investment in mutual funds is not like what we think. The world of mutual fund investment has many sides and goes beyond the simple act of putting money into a fund, it needs a complete understanding of several factors that can influence the performance and outcome of your investment.

In the vast landscape of financial instruments, Mutual Funds stand as a beacon of accessibility, offering investors a dynamic and diversified approach to wealth creation. Whether you are a seasoned investor seeking to optimize your portfolio or a novice navigating the complex world of finance, believe me, this book is your road map to understand and harness the power of mutual funds.

Let me tell you a short story:

There was a person named John. John likes to visit different countries every year. He has been doing this for more than 9 years. But he notices that the cost of his vacations goes up each year. He is confused, after searching on Google he learned about inflation.

Looking at his savings, he sees that his money is not growing as fast as the cost of his vacations. He thinks, "If my vacation gets 7.66% more expensive each year and my money grows only by 3%, I won't be able to afford them soon!"

He decides, "That's it! I will not stand for this!" and goes to his friend Mike's house. John explains the inflation thing and he realizes Mike is dealing with the same issue. They decide to do something about it.

They find 8 other friends facing the same problem and have a big group call. Together they came up with a SUPERB IDEA of investing in mutual funds.

So, they all joined their money together and hired a "Money Manager" to take care of it. The Money Manager split the whole pile into 10 parts and gave one part to each friend. Then the Money Manager used this money to buy lots of different things called shares and bonds.

After one year, those shares and bonds did some magic and made a return of 20%. All 10 friends were super happy because all of their money grew by 20%. John was especially relieved because now he knew he would not run out of money for his travels ever again. And then all lived happily ever after, thanks to their clever Money Manager and the magic of shares and bonds.

The "Pool" of money that is invested in different stocks or bonds is called a FUND.

The "Money Manager" who manages other people's money in real life is called a FUND MANAGER.

WHAT IS A MUTUAL FUND?

Many investors have confusion in their minds. They think a Mutual Fund is an investment company for financial instruments or something like it.

I would say, there is no specific definition that is universally accepted for mutual funds.

Let us check some definitions by renowned organizations:

As per SEBI (Mutual Funds) Regulations, 1996, Chapter 1 Definitions – "Mutual fund means a fund established in the form of a trust to raise monies through the sales of units to the public or a section of the public or a section of the public under one or more schemes for investing in securities including money market instruments or gold or gold related instruments or real estate assets."

As per the SEC (Securities and Exchange Commission) Definition – "A mutual fund is a company that brings together money from many people and invests it in stocks bonds or other assets. The combined holding of stocks, bonds, or other assets the fund owns is known as its portfolio. Each investor in the fund owns a share which represents a part of these holdings."

As per Wikipedia – "A mutual fund is an open-end professionally managed investment fund that pulls the money from many investors to purchase securities. These investors may be in retail or institutional. The term is typically used in the United States, while similar structures across the globe include the SICAV in Europe (Investment Company with variable capital) and open-ended investment company (OEIC) in the UK."

I am sure that you are now confused with the above definitions but don't worry, I'll explain it in very simple words.

Remember that!

MUTUAL FUND =

MANY PEOPLE'S MONEY + PROFESSIONAL MANAGER

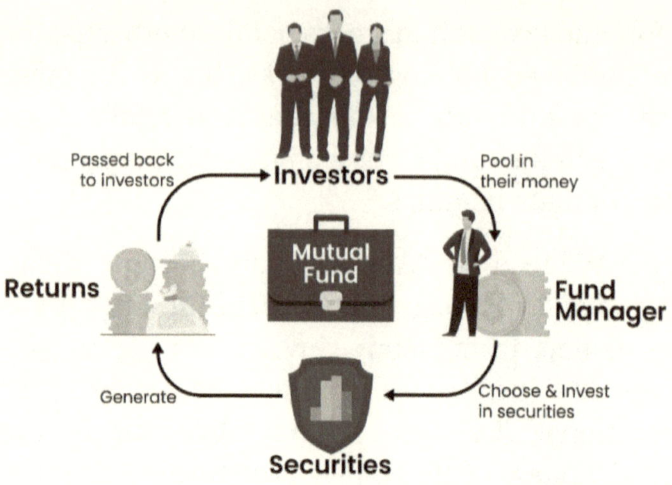

Imagine you and a bunch of friends, each putting some money together to buy a variety of things like toys, snacks, and games. Now, instead of everyone deciding what to buy you hire a friend who is good at picking awesome stuff. That friend is like the professional manager of your shared money.

So, a mutual fund is like a big Piggy Bank where lots of people pool their money, and a professional manager decides where to invest that money to make it grow. Everyone shares in the gains and losses, depending on how the investments do. It's like a team effort to make everyone's money grow without each person having to be an expert in picking the right things to invest in!

Key Takeaway is "A mutual fund is an investment vehicle that pools money from multiple investors to purchase a diversified portfolio of stocks, bonds, or other securities. Managed by professional fund managers, mutual funds offer a convenient way for individuals to access a diverse range of assets without directly managing them. Investors buy shares in the mutual fund, and their returns or losses are proportional to the fund's performance. Mutual funds provide diversification, professional management, and liquidity to investors."

With mutual funds, you can invest in a range of companies and sectors without needing to pick individual stocks. It's like having a team of experts doing the research for you.

WHY SHOULD YOU INVEST IN MUTUAL FUNDS?

Normally people think that investing in Fixed Deposits or Gold is more secure than investing in mutual funds.

But if you ask me my opinion, investing in mutual funds is one of the safest ways to invest for the long term. Let me explain why. Investing in mutual funds can offer diverse benefits, and here are the top 10 reasons why many people choose to include mutual funds in their investment portfolios:

1. Easy Diversification

Mutual funds pull money from multiple investors to invest in a variety of securities, such as stocks, bonds, and other assets. This diversification helps spread risk, reducing the impact of poor performance in any single investment.

2. Expert Management

Mutual funds are managed by professional fund managers who make investment decisions based on in-depth research and market analysis. This expertise can be beneficial for investors who may not have the time or knowledge to manage their investments actively.

3. Affordability

Mutual funds allow investors to participate in a diversified portfolio with a relatively small investment amount. This makes it accessible to a wide range of investors, including those with limited capital.

4. Flexibility

Mutual funds are generally liquid, meaning investors can buy or sell shares on any business day at the current net asset value (NAV). This liquidity provides flexibility for investors who may need to access their money quickly.

5. Options for Everyone

There is a wide range of mutual fund options, including equity funds, bond funds, money market funds, index funds, and hybrid funds. Investors can choose funds that align with their financial goals, risk tolerance, and investment preferences.

6. Automatic Reinvestment

Many mutual funds offer automatic dividends and capital gains reinvestments, allowing investors to compound their returns by automatically reinvesting earned income.

7. Regular Updates

Financial authorities regulate mutual funds to ensure transparency and protect the interests of investors. In many countries, regulatory bodies like the Securities and Exchange Commission (SEC) provide oversight.

8. Safe and Regulated

Investing in mutual funds is convenient and accessible. Investors can buy and sell shares through various channels, including online platforms, financial advisors, and fund companies.

9. Regular Reporting

Mutual funds provide regular updates and statements, keeping investors informed about their holdings, performance, and any income distributions. This transparency allows investors to monitor the progress of their investments.

10. Potential for higher returns

While returns are not guaranteed, mutual funds offer the potential for higher returns compared to traditional savings accounts or fixed deposits. The diversified nature of mutual funds can contribute to better risk-adjusted returns over the long term.

HISTORY OF MUTUAL FUNDS IN INDIA

Now let's understand a little bit about the history of mutual funds.

For a country to become strong and well-developed, it needs a good financial system where many people take part. In India, they took a big step towards this in 1963 by creating the first mutual fund called Unit Trust of India (UTI). The government and the Reserve Bank of India started it to encourage people to save, invest, and join in the benefits of the money earned from buying, holding, managing, and selling securities.

In recent years, mutual funds in India have become much bigger. The story of mutual funds in India has five main parts or phases.

First phase - 1964 to 1987

Mutual funds in India began in 1963 with the creation of the UTI (Unit Trust of India) by a law passed by the government. At first, the Reserve Bank of India (RBI) managed it. In 1978, it became independent from the RBI, and the Industrial Development Bank of India (IDBI) took over. The first plan it offered was called Unit Scheme 1964 (US'64). By the end of 1988, UTI had rupees 6700 crores worth of things it was managing for people, which are called assets under management (AUM).

Second phase - 1987 to 1993

In 1987, things changed in the world of mutual funds in India. Before that, it was mostly managed by one big fund called UTI. But in 1987, other big organizations like public sector banks, Life Insurance Corporation of India (LIC), and General Insurance Corporation of India (GIC) joined in. SBI mutual fund was the first to start in June 1987 followed by the Canbank mutual fund (Dec 1987), the Punjab National Bank mutual fund (Aug 1989), the Indian Bank mutual fund (Nov 1989), Bank of India (June 1990), Bank of Baroda mutual fund (Oct 1992). LIC started its mutual fund in June 1989, and GIC began in December 1990. By the end of 1993, all these mutual funds together were managing rupees 47,004 crores.

Third phase - 1993 to 2003

In April 1992, a group called SEBI started to look after the Indian securities market. Their job was to make sure people who invested in the market were safe and to help the market grow.

Then, in 1993, SEBI made rules for mutual funds (except UTI). Kothari Pioneer (which is now part of Franklin Templeton Mutual Fund) was the first private mutual fund to follow these rules in July 1993. This was a big deal because it opened the door for more private companies to offer different kinds of mutual funds to Indian investors.

As the years went by, more mutual funds started and even companies from other countries joined in. There were also some mergers and buyouts in the mutual fund world. By January 2003, there were 33 mutual funds in India, managing a total of rupees 1,21,805 crores. UTI alone managed rupees 44,541 crores of that money.

Fourth phase 2003 to 2014

In February 2003, the rules for UTI (Unit Trust of India) changed. UTI was split into two parts - one was called the Specified Undertaking of the Unit Trust of India (SUUTI), and the other part was the UTI Mutual Fund. UTI Mutual Fund started following new rules made by SEBI. With this change and some joining together of private mutual funds, the mutual fund world in India went through a big shift.

In 2009, the world had a big financial problem, and it affected India too. Many people who had put money in the market when it was doing well lost money, and they didn't trust mutual funds as much. SEBI, the group that looks after these things, also removed something called "Entry Load" which added to the challenges for mutual funds. Because of all these issues, the Indian mutual fund world had a tough time growing between 2010 and 2013.

Fifth Phase (Current) Since 2014

To help mutual funds reach more people, especially in smaller cities, SEBI (the group overseeing these things) made some important changes in September 2012. These changes aimed to make mutual funds more popular and get more people interested.

After these changes, things started getting better for the mutual fund world, especially when a new government came into power. Since May 2014, more and more people started putting money into mutual funds. By May 2014, the total amount of money managed by mutual funds crossed rupees 10 trillion (Rupees 10 Lakh Crore), and in just three years, it doubled and reached Rupees 20 trillion (Rupees 20 Lakh Crore) in August 2017. By November 2020, it went even higher, crossing Rupees 30 trillion (30 Lakh Crore).

Overall, in the last 10 years, the size of the Indian mutual fund world has grown more than five times, from Rupees 8.34 trillion in October 2013 to Rupees 46.72 trillion in October 2023. In the last five years alone, the money managed by mutual funds more than doubled from Rupees 22.24 trillion in October 2018 to Rupees 46.72 trillion in October 2023

More and more people are also becoming part of mutual funds. The number of investor's accounts went up from 7.90 crore in October 2018 to 15.96 crore in October 2023, which is more than a double increase in five years. On average, 13.44 lakh new investor accounts have been added every month since October 2018.

This growth happened because of some rules SEBI made in 2012 and the support from people who help others invest, called mutual fund distributors. These distributors play a crucial role, especially in smaller towns, by helping people invest and guiding them through the ups and downs in the market.

Mutual Fund distributors have also played a big part in making systematic investment plans (SIPs) popular. In April 2016, the number of SIP accounts crossed 1 crore, and as of October 2023, there are 7.30 crore SIP accounts.

> Investing is not about getting rich quick; it's about building wealth over time.
>
> — David Bach

STRUCTURE OF MUTUAL FUND

I hope you understand what a massive change has happened in the mutual fund industry from 1964 to 2023. Now let's understand the structure of the mutual fund and its key elements.

The structure of a mutual fund involves several key components and entities that work together to manage and operate the fund.

Here are the main elements of a mutual fund structure:

Sponsor:

This Sponsor is the entity that establishes the mutual fund. It could be a financial institution, bank, or any other corporate body. The Sponsor creates the mutual fund and registers it with the regulatory authorities.

Trust:

In the case of a mutual fund, the Sponsor creates trust. The trust is responsible for holding the assets of the fund for the benefit of the unit holders (investors).

Trustees:

Trustees are responsible for overseeing the operations of the mutual fund and ensuring that it complies with all regulatory requirements. They act in the interest of the unit holders.

Asset Management Company (AMC):

The trustees appoint the AMC to manage the investments of the mutual fund. It is responsible for making investment decisions, buying and selling securities, and overall portfolio management.

Custodian:

The Custodian is responsible for holding and safeguarding the securities and assets of the mutual fund. They play a crucial role in ensuring the security and integrity of the fund's holdings.

Registrar and Transfer Agent (RTA):

The RTA is responsible for maintaining the records of the investors, processing translations (purchases, redemptions, etc.), and managing other administrative tasks related to investor services.

Distributors:

Distributors are individuals or entities that help in selling mutual fund units to investors. They may receive a commission or fee for their services.

Investors (Unit Holders):

Investors, also known as Unit Holders, are individuals or entities that invest more in the mutual fund by purchasing units. The units represent the investor's proportionate share of the fund's assets.

SEBI (Securities and Exchange Board of India):

SEBI is the regulatory authority that oversees and regulates mutual funds in India. It establishes rules and guidelines to ensure the protection of investors and the proper functioning of mutual funds.

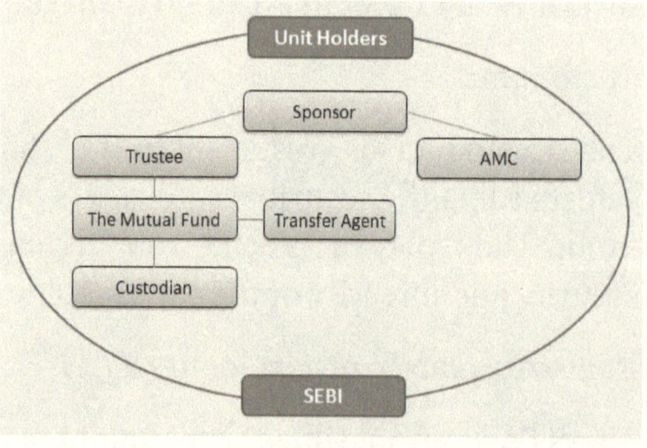

The flow of operations typically involves Investors buying units from the fund, the AMC managing the fund's investments, the Custodian holding the fund's assets, and the Trustees overseeing the entire process to ensure compliance with regulations and the best interests of the investors.

HOW ARE RETURNS MADE IN A MUTUAL FUND?

A mutual fund puts money into a mix of things like stocks and bonds. When the prices of these things go up (like for stocks or when the fund earns interest from bonds), the mutual fund becomes more valuable. If the prices of stocks or bonds go down, the value of the mutual fund also goes down. So, when the mutual fund becomes more valuable the money you put into it also increases.

1. When you decide to sell your mutual fund, you might make some money, and that's called a CAPITAL GAIN. Capital gain is like the profit you get from selling your mutual fund units. It's the extra money you make because the value of your units has gone up. You calculate it by finding the difference between how much your units are worth when you sell them and how much you pay for them. If you sell them for less than you paid, that's called a CAPITAL LOSS.

2. When your mutual fund gives you money, it's called earning dividends. This happens when the Mutual fund decides to share some of the profits it made. These profits can be from selling things like stocks for a profit, making interest from bonds, or getting dividends from stocks. So, when the mutual fund makes extra money, they might share some of it with you, and that's your DIVIDEND. It is also called as Income Distribution Cum Capital Withdrawal (IDCW).

IDCW vs Growth Options

Now I know the question that comes to your mind is what is the difference between IDCW and Capital Gain/Growth option?

Let me tell you the difference, in mutual funds there are two choices –

One is where the mutual fund gives you a part of the money it makes. You get this extra money regularly, like every month or every three months. When you get this extra money, the total value of your investment goes down a bit. This is called the IDCW option.

Second is when the mutual fund takes the money it makes and puts it back into your investment. You don't get extra money regularly. Instead, your total investment value keeps going up over time. Your investment grows because the money it earns is added back to it. It's like letting your money make more money over the years.

Types of IDCW:

IDCW is a term used for a specific option provided by the mutual fund in India. It primarily applies to open-ended mutual fund schemes. There are two types of IDCW in mutual funds.

Payout Option:

Under the IDCW payout option, the mutual fund distributes the income generated by the fund dividends and interest income to the investors. The distribution is made at regular intervals, typically monthly, quarterly, or annually. Investors choosing this option receive a regular stream of income from the mutual fund.

Imagine you have a box of chocolates that represents the mutual fund. With the payout option, the mutual fund regularly gives you some chocolate (income) from the box. You enjoy them as a treat, and this happens at set times.

Reinvestment Option:

The IDCW reinvestment option involves reinvesting the income distribution back into the mutual fund. Instead of receiving the income in cash, investors opt for this option which automatically reinvests the distributed amount by acquiring more units of the mutual fund. This can help in the compounding of returns over time.

To continue the above example, imagine that now with the reinvestment option instead of giving you chocolates to enjoy, the mutual fund takes those chocolates (income) and puts them back into your box. So, your box gets a bit bigger over time as you keep adding more chocolates to it.

These options are like choosing how you want to enjoy the benefits from your mutual fund either by receiving regular treats (payouts) or by letting your collection grow over time (reinvestment). It depends on what you pay for and what suits your financial goals.

So, again another question that comes to your mind is which one to choose.

Remember, it depends on what you want - regular extra money (IDCW) or letting your investment grow over time (Growth).

The best time to plant a mutual fund tree was 20 years ago. The second-best time is now.

Regular and Direct options:

In the "Regular" option, investors typically go through intermediaries such as brokers, financial advisors, or distributors to invest in mutual funds. These intermediaries provide advice and assistance to investors and, in return, receive a Commission or fee from the mutual fund company. The Commission is usually embedded in the expense ratio of the mutual fund.

On the other hand, the "Direct" option allows investors to bypass intermediaries and invest directly with the mutual fund company. This means investors deal directly with the fund house without involving a distributor. Because there is no intermediary involved, the expenses are usually lower in the direct option compared to the regular option.

	Direct	Regular
Costs	It is less expensive because of no intermediary.	Relatively higher as intermediaries are included.
Returns	Lower expense higher return.	Lower return compared to the Direct option.

	An investor need to make investment decisions on their own.	Investors may receive guidance and recommendations from financial advisors/distributors.
Investor Involvement		
Choice of Funds	Both Direct and Regular options offer access to the same Mutual Funds.	

Let's understand this concept through a Short Story. The tale of two choices in the magical investment Kingdom:

In a land where coins grew on trees, there was a magical investment Kingdom with two gates leading to wealth - the regular gate and the direct gate.

Regular Gate:

Meet Sarah, a curious adventure. She entered the Regular Gate, where a wise guide named Advisor AI greeted her. Sarah wanted to plant her money in the enchanted mutual fund forest. Advisor AI, with his knowledge, recommended the ABC wealth tree, and Sarah happily invested.

Yet, every time the ABC wealth tree bore its magical fruits, a tiny portion was shared with advisor AI as a gesture of thanks for his guidance. Sarah got her share, though slightly less than the full bounty of the enchanted fruits.

Direct Gate:

Meanwhile, Jake, or determined explorer, chose the Direct Gate. He bypassed advisor AI and went straight to the mutual fund castle, where the mutual fund wizard, Emma, managed the ABC wealth tree. Jake, armed with research, directly invested in the ABC wealth tree without the aid of a guide.

Since Jake didn't share his fruits with any advisor, he received the complete harvest of the magical fruits. It was a tad more than what Sarah got through the regular gate.

The lesson from the magical investment Kingdom:

In the end, both Sarah and Jake enjoy the wealth of the enchanted trees. Sarah took the scenic route through the regular gate, appreciating the guidance of advisor AI. Jake, the self-sufficient adventurer, opted for the direct gate and enjoyed a slightly larger share of the magical fruits.

The magical investment Kingdom taught them that in the world of enchanted wheels, there are different gates to choose from, one with a guide to assist and one where you navigate independently. Your choice depends on your adventure style and whether you prefer the wisdom of a guide or a direct path to the enchanted wealth castle.

Now I hope you can understand the difference between Direct and Regular investment.

HOW TO DO BANK ANALYSIS?

Let's imagine a conversation between three friends – Alex, Bailey, and Casey - as they discuss their investment plans. Each friend has a unique perspective and approach to investing. They started the conversation by suggesting the idea of setting clear financial goals. Alex said that he received a return of 3% by investing in savings accounts. Bailey said she received 6% by investing in fixed deposits. However, Alex is a careful planner in the group. He said that he received around 25% return by investing in the stock market.

Is it that easy to get a good return by investing in stocks?

The answer is 'Yes' but one needs to be incredibly careful and complete the study about investing in any banks or mutual funds.

Here we will understand how to perform the Bank Analysis of banks or Non-Banking Financial Companies (NBFC) like Muthoot Finance, Manapuram Finance, and many more.

Non-Banking Finance Company (NBFC)

Imagine you have a friend named Finance Freddy. Now, Freddy doesn't work at a traditional bank, but he does something very similar.

Freddy is not a bank, but he does financial stuff like a bank. He gives out loans, helps people buy things, and deals with money matters.

If you need money to buy a new bicycle, you can go to Freddy. He might give you a loan, and then you can pay him back in small amounts over time. It's like getting a loan from a bank, but Freddy is not a bank.

Freddy also helps people buy expensive things like refrigerators or laptops. If you can't pay for these all at once, he might let you pay in installments, making it easier for you.

Unlike traditional banks, Freddy doesn't have to follow all the same strict rules. But he still has to make sure he's fair and trustworthy because he's dealing with people's money.

Freddy might also help you invest money or set up a savings plan. Even though he's not a bank, he can still assist with these financial activities.

The term non-banking just means Freddy is not exactly a bank. He doesn't take deposits like a regular bank does.

So, the takeaway is that "Non-Banking Finance Companies" (NBFC) like Finance Freddy, are financial entities that provide services similar to banks, such as giving out loans, helping with purchases, and offering financial services. They are not banks, but they play a similar role in helping people with their money matters.

Advances Growth

It means the bank is giving out more loans or credit to people and businesses. This is often a good thing because it shows the bank is helping the economy by supporting investments and purchases. More loans mean the bank is lending more money to customers. This money can be used for various things like buying a home, starting a business, or other important stuff.

Lending money is how the bank makes a lot of its own money. The interest people pay on loans adds up, and that's income for the bank. When a bank is giving out more loans, it often means people and businesses are active in the economy. They are borrowing money for different reasons, which can be a sign of a healthy and growing economy.

While more lending is generally good, the bank must be careful about who they lend to. Too much lending to risky customers can cause problems. Banks have rules they need to follow while lending money. The government keeps an eye on these to make sure everything is fair and safe for everyone.

So, when you hear about a bank's "advances growth" it is like saying the bank is helping more people and businesses by lending them money, and that's usually a positive sign for the economy.

If the Bank lent more to their customers, is a good sign because the bank will receive more interest for the amount they lent to the customers.

> A higher 'Advances Growth' value is considered better.

Net Interest Income (NII)

Net interest income is a key measure for banks and financial institutions. It represents the difference between the interest earned by the bank through its lending activities like loan mortgages etcetera and the interest paid on its borrowings (like deposits or funds borrowed from other banks).

Imagine you have a lemonade stand and decide to lend money to your friends to help them set up their lemonade stand. You charge them a little extra interest when they pay you back.

Lending Money (Earning Interest):

You lend ₹10 to your friend Amy, and she promises to pay you back ₹12 next month. You have earned ₹2 in interest (₹12 - ₹10).

Lending to Others:

You do the same with two more friends. Bob borrows ₹15 and promises to pay back ₹18, earning you ₹3 in interest. Cindy borrows ₹20 and promises you back ₹24, earning you ₹4 in interest.

Total interest Earned:

Now, you add up all the interest earned: ₹2 (from Amy) + ₹3 (from Bob) ₹4 (from Cindy) = ₹9.

Borrowing Money (Paying Interest):

To keep your lemonade cold, you need ice. You borrow ₹5 from your neighbor and agree to pay him back ₹6 next month. You have paid ₹1 in Interest (₹6 - ₹5).

Calculating net Interest Income:

To find your Net Interest Income, you subtract the interest you paid for the ice (₹1) from the total interest you earned (₹9). So, your Net Interest Income is ₹8 (₹9 - ₹1).

In the real banking world, instead of lending lemonade stand money, banks lend actual money.

Net Interest Income is the difference between the interest earned from loans (like your friends paying you back with extra money) and the interest paid on deposits on borrowed funds (like you paying interest for the ice).

So, the summary is that Net Interest Income (NII) is the money a bank makes by lending after considering the cost of borrowing. It's a crucial measure of a bank's core lending and borrowing profitability.

A higher 'Net Interest Income' value is considered better.

Net Interest Margin (NIM)

Consider the same lemonade example we discussed in the previous topic, you have a lemonade stand bank, and you lend lemonade to friends who want to set up their own stands. When they pay you back, they give you a little extra lemonade as a thank you (interest).

Your friends pay you interest, but you also need to borrow some ice to keep your lemonade cold, right? So, the ice supplier charges you a small fee (interest) for lending you that ice.

Net Interest Margin is like figuring out how much extra lemonade you have after considering the lemonade you earned from lending and the lemonade you spent on borrowing ice.

Let's say you earn 5 extra cups of lemonade from lending and pay 1 cup for the borrowed ice. Your Net Interest Margin (NIM) is 4 cups (5 cups - 1 cup).

In the real banking world, instead of lemonade, banks deal with money. Net Interest Margin is the difference between the interest earned from loans (like your friends paying you back with extra money) and the interest paid on deposits or borrowed funds (like you paying interest for the ice). It is calculated in percentages.

So, the takeaway is that Net Interest Margin (NIM) helps banks understand how much money they make from their lending activities after considering the cost of borrowing. It's like figuring out the extra profit margin from the interest earned on loans compared to the interest paid on funds borrowed.

A higher 'Net Interest Margin' value is considered better.

Non-Performing Assets (NPA)

Now you understand that banks lend money to individuals and businesses. Non-performing assets are loans where the borrowers are not repaying as agreed, which can cause financial challenges for the bank.

So, the non-performing assets are like loans that are not working well for a bank because people are not repaying them on time or in good condition. It's an important aspect for banks to manage to ensure their financial health, just like you need to keep an eye on your cups for a successful lemonade stand.

A lower 'Non-Performing Assets' value is considered better.

CASA Ratio

CA is a Current Account, like putting money directly into your Piggy Bank. It's like when you get some cash and immediately drop it into your Piggy Bank. The money is ready for you to use whenever you want.

SA is a Savings Account, like a promise to put money into your Piggy Bank later. It's like when your friend owes you some money, and he promises to give it to you later. You know it's coming, but it's not in your piggy bank right away.

So, the Casa ratio calculation is how much of your total money in the Piggy Bank is from the current account (money in hand) and how much is from the savings account (promised money).

Let's say you have ₹100 in your Piggy Bank. ₹60 is from the current account (money in hand), and ₹40 is from the savings account (promised money). Your CASA ratio is then calculated as ₹60 (Current Account) divided by ₹100 (Total Money), which is 0.6 or 60%.

In the banking world, the Casa ratio is measured by how much the bank's total deposits come from the Current Account (money in hand) and Savings Account (promised money). A higher CASA ratio is often seen as good for a bank.

CASA ratio is like looking at the mix of immediate use money (Current Account) and promised money (Savings Account) in a bank. It helps banks understand how much of their deposits are readily available for use.

A higher 'CASA Ratio" value is considered better.

For better understanding, I have created a table with all key takeaways from the above particulars.

Particulars	Good or Bad
Advances Growth	Higher the better
Net Interest Income	Higher the better
Net Interest Margin	Higher the better
Non-Performing Asset	Lower the better
CASA Ratio	Higher the better

Let's compare and check these particulars with an actual example of SBI Q2 FY22 and Q2 FY23:

Particulars	Q2 FY22	Q2 FY23	Y-O-Y change
Gross Advances (in Cr.)	25,30,777	3035,071	19.93%
NII (in Cr.)	31,184	35,183	12.83%
NIM	3.5%	3.55%	5 bps
Net NPA	1.52%	0.80%	-72 bps
CASA (in Cr.)	17,06,387	17,97,752	5.35%

In this table, we compared SBI Q2 FY23 with SBI Q2 FY22. Q2 means the Second Quarter i.e., July to September. Y-O-Y change is a Year-On-Year change that shows the changes for the defined Quarter.

Gross Advances: The Bank gave loans/credit to people or businesses is ₹25,30,777 Cr. in Q2 FY22 and 30,35,071 Cr. in Q2 FY23 which means the bank gave almost 20% more loans in Q2 FY23 which is a good sign.

Net Interest Income (NII): The difference between Interest earned and paid is ₹31,184 Cr. in Q2 FY22 and 35,183 Cr. in Q2 FY23 which means the Interest earned is 12.83% more in Q2 FY23 which is a good sign.

Net Interest Margin (NIM): It is 3.50% in Q2 FY22 and Q2 FY23 which shows a positive change of 0.05% (5 bps) in Q2 FY23.

Net NPA: It is 1.52% in Q2 FY22 and 0.80% in Q2 FY23 which means the percentage is reduced in Q2 FY23 by -72 bps which is a good sign.

CASA: It is 17,06,387 Cr. in Q2 FY22 and 17,97,752 Cr. in Q2 FY23 which shows an increase of 5.35% in Q2 FY23 which is a good sign.

> Do your research before investing in any mutual fund. Pay attention to the fees, the investment style, and the track record.
>
> - Suze Orman

MUTUAL FUND CATEGORIES

Now let's understand what the mutual fund categories are. Mutual funds are categorized based on the types of assets they invest in, their investment objectives, and risk profiles.

Let's see the list of funds as of the year 2023.

I tried to list as many funds as I could find. Remember that the availability and performance of mutual funds can change frequently. These funds might be renamed, modified, or closed over time. The below list shows Debt Funds, Equity Funds, Hybrid Funds, Commodity Funds, and Other Funds.

Debt Funds:

1. Floating Rate Fund
2. Banding & PSU Fund
3. Ultra Short Duration Fund
4. Medium Duration Fund

5. Flexi Maturity Fund
6. Money Market Fund
7. Overnight Fund
8. Credit Risk Fund
9. Dynamic Bond Fund
10. Liquid Fund
11. Corporate Bond Fund
12. Low Duration Fund
13. Gilt-Long Term Fund
14. Short Duration Fund
15. Sectorial Fund Infrastructure
16. Long Duration Fund
17. Gilt – Short & Mid-Term Fund
18. Medium to Long Duration Fund
19. Debt – Interval Fund

Debt Mutual Funds, the Anchor of Stability in Your Investment Portfolio, Balancing Risk and Reward for Steady Financial Growth.

Equity Funds:

1. Thematic Fund
2. Focus Fund
3. Large & Mid Cap Fund
4. Index Fund
5. Large Cap Fund

6. Contra Fund
7. Flexi Cap Fund
8. Thematic Fund – Global
9. Mid-Cap Fund
10. Small Cap Fund
11. Equity Link Saving Scheme
12. Sectorial Fund – Pharma & Health Care
13. Thematic Fund – MNC
14. Value Fund
15. Sectorial Fund – Consumption
16. Multi Cap Fund
17. Sectorial Fund – Infrastructure
18. Dividend Yield Fund
19. Sectorial Fund – Service Industry
20. Sectorial Fund – Bank & Financial Services
21. Sectorial Fund - Technology
22. Sectorial Fund - Energy & Power
23. Sectorial Fund – Auto

> Equity Mutual Funds, the Engine of Wealth Creation, Accelerating Your Financial Journey with the Power of Growth and Opportunity

Commodity Funds:

1. FoFs – Gold
2. Flexi Cap Fund

Hybrid Funds:

1. Arbitrate Fund
2. Multi Asset Allocation Fund
3. Balanced Advantage Fund
4. Aggressive Advantage Fund
5. Dynamic Asset Allocation Fund
6. Equity Savings
7. Conservative Hybrid Fund
8. Balanced Hybrid Fund

Hybrid Mutual Funds, Your Adaptive Financial Ally, Striking the Perfect Balance Between Stability and Growth for a Resilient Investment Strategy.

Other Funds:

1. FoFs (Domestic) – Equity Oriented
2. Solution-Oriented – Children's Fund
3. FoFs – Overseas
4. FoFs (Domestic) – Debt Oriented
5. Solution Oriented – Retirement Fund
6. Flexi Cap Fund

I have explained the composition, risk factors, and suitable horizon for some of the popular funds in the market.

Debt Funds

Banking and PSU Fund:

A banking and PSU fund is a type of debt mutual fund in India that primarily invests in debt instruments issued by banks, public sector undertakings (PSUs), and public financial institutions.

These funds aim to provide relatively safe and stable investment options, with a lower risk profile compared to other debt funds.

The portfolio is composed of high-quality debt securities, making it suitable for conservative investors seeking regular income and capital preservation first off while they may be sensitive to interest rate movements, the impact is typically lower, and the funds are considered suitable for those with shorter investment horizons.

Short Duration Fund:

A short-duration fund is a type of debt mutual fund that invests in fixed-income securities with a relatively short maturity, typically ranging from 1 to 3 years.

These funds aim to provide stable returns while minimizing interest rate risk.

The shorter duration helps reduce sensitivity to interest rate fluctuations, making them suitable for investors seeking a balance between income and capital preservation with a moderate risk profile.

Short-duration funds may invest in a mix of government and corporate bonds, offering a potential source of regular income with lower volatility compared to longer-duration debt funds.

Ultra Short Duration Fund:

An ultra-short-duration fund is a type of debt mutual fund that primarily invests in very short-term fixed-income securities, typically with maturities ranging from a few days to a few months.

The key features include low interest rate sensitivity, high liquidity, and a focus on capital preservation.

These funds aimed to offer stability, making them suitable for conservative investors with a short to ultra-short investment horizon.

They provide a balance between regular income and low volatility, making them an alternative to traditional savings accounts or short-term deposits.

Medium Duration Fund:

A Medium Duration Fund is a type of debt mutual fund that primarily invests in fixed-income securities with a moderate duration, typically ranging from three to four years.

These funds aim to strike a balance between generating higher returns than short-term funds while managing interest rate risk more effectively than long-term funds.

Medium Duration Funds are suitable for investors with a moderate risk appetite and a slightly longer investment horizon.

They may invest in a mix of government and corporate bonds to provide a combination of income and potential capital appreciation.

Low Duration Fund:

A low-duration Fund is a type of debt mutual fund that primarily invests in short to ultra-short-term fixed-income securities, typically with a maturity of up to six months.

These funds aim to offer a balance between generating income and minimizing interest rate risk.

With a focus on shorter-duration securities, low-duration funds provide lower sensitivity to interest rate fluctuations compared to medium or long-duration funds.

They are suitable for conservative investors seeking stability, liquidity, and a slightly higher return than very short-term funds.

Long Duration Fund:

A long-duration Fund is a type of debt mutual fund that primarily invests in fixed-income securities with a longer maturity period, typically exceeding seven years.

These funds aim to capitalize on potential higher returns from long-term bonds but come with higher interest rate risk.

Long-duration Funds are suitable for investors with a higher risk tolerance and a longer investment horizon.

They may experience greater volatility in response to changes in interest rates. These funds can provide higher income potential but require careful consideration of interest rate trends and potential impact on the fund's returns.

Liquid Fund:

A Liquid Fund is a type of mutual fund that invests in short-term, highly liquid debt instruments.

It focuses on short-maturity securities, providing easy access to funds for investors. With a goal of capital preservation and stability, liquid funds are considered low-risk and suitable for short-term parking of funds or emergency cash needs.

They aim to generate regular income through interest on short-term instruments, making them an alternative to traditional savings accounts with the added benefit of potentially higher returns.

Corporate Bond Fund:

A corporate bond Fund is a mutual fund that invests in bonds issued by corporations.

It aims to provide regular income through interest payments. The fund holds a diversified portfolio of corporate bonds, spreading risk.

While it carries a higher risk than government bond funds, it also offers the potential for higher returns.

Investors choose corporate bond funds based on their risk tolerance and income goals, making them a balanced option for those seeking a mix of income and moderate risk.

Medium to Long Duration Fund:

A Medium-to-Long Duration Fund is a type of debt mutual fund that invests in fixed-income securities with a medium-to-long maturity period.

It aims to strike a balance between generating higher returns compared to short-term funds and managing interest rate risk more effectively than long-term funds.

These funds are suitable for investors with a moderate risk appetite and a medium to long-term investment horizon.

Dynamic Bond Fund:

A Dynamic Bond Fund is a type of mutual fund that dynamically adjusts its portfolio composition based on changing market conditions, interest rate outlook, and credit risk assessments.

The fund manager has the flexibility to invest across various fixed-income instruments, including government securities, corporate bonds, and other debt instruments.

The objective is to optimize returns by actively managing the fund's duration and credit exposure.

Dynamic Bond Funds are suitable for investors seeking a flexible fixed-income investment that can adapt to evolving market scenarios.

Gilt Fund:

A Gilt Fund is a type of mutual fund that primarily invests in government securities, providing investors with a low-risk option.

These funds focus on bonds and treasury bills issued by the government, offering the safety of capital and regular income through interest payments.

While they have minimal credit risk, Gilt Funds can be sensitive to changes in interest rates, impacting on their returns.

They are suitable for conservative investors seeking stability in their fixed-income investments.

Equity Funds

Index Fund:

An Index Fund is a type of mutual fund or exchange-traded fund (ETF) that aims to replicate the performance of a specific market index, such as the S&P 500.

Instead of actively selecting individual stocks, the fund invests in a diversified portfolio that mirrors the composition of the chosen index.

The goal is to provide investors with returns that closely match the overall market performance represented by the selected index.

Index funds are known for their passivity, lower management fees, and broad market exposure, making them a popular choice for investors seeking a simple and cost-effective way to invest in the broader market.

All banks and financial institutions offer this fund however, one should do a bank analysis before choosing any Index Fund.

Large Cap Fund:

A Large-Cap Fund is a type of mutual fund or exchange-traded fund (ETF) that primarily invests in stocks of large-cap companies.

Large cap refers to companies with a high market capitalization, indicating that they are generally well-established and have a significant presence in the market.

Large-cap funds aim to provide investors with exposure to the stability and established track records of these larger companies.

They are considered relatively less volatile compared to mid and small-cap funds, making them suitable for investors seeking a more stable investment with potentially moderate returns.

Mid Cap Fund:

A Mid-Cap Fund is a type of mutual fund or exchange-traded fund (ETF) that primarily invests in stocks of mid-sized companies.

Mid-cap refers to companies with a moderate market capitalization, falling between large-cap and small-cap.

These funds aim to provide investors with exposure to the growth potential and dynamism of mid-sized companies.

Mid-cap funds are generally considered to have higher growth potential than large-cap funds, but they also come with a higher level of risk and volatility.

They are suitable for investors seeking a balance between the stability of large-cap investments and the growth potential of small-cap stocks.

Small Cap Fund:

A Small-Cap Fund is a type of mutual fund or exchange-traded fund (ETF) that primarily invests in stocks of small-sized companies.

Small cap refers to companies with a relatively low market capitalization.

These funds aim to provide investors with exposure to the growth potential and higher volatility associated with smaller companies.

Small-cap funds are considered riskier than large and mid-cap funds, but they also offer the potential for higher returns.

They are suitable for investors seeking more aggressive growth opportunities and are willing to accept a higher level of risk in their investment portfolio.

Large & Mid Cap Fund:

A Large & Mid Cap Fund is a type of mutual fund that invests in a mix of both large-cap and mid-cap stocks.

Large-cap stocks are from well-established, larger companies, while mid-cap stocks are from companies with moderate market capitalization.

These funds aim to provide investors with a balanced portfolio, combining the stability of large-cap stocks with the growth potential of mid-cap stocks.

This diversification strategy offers a compromise between stability and potential returns, making Large & Mid Cap Funds suitable for investors seeking a balanced and diversified equity investment.

Multi Cap Fund:

A Multi-Cap Fund is a type of mutual fund that invests across various market capitalizations, including large-cap, mid-cap, and small-cap stocks.

This provides investors with a diversified portfolio covering companies of different sizes. Multi-cap funds offer flexibility for fund managers to adjust the allocation based on market conditions, seeking a balance between stability and growth potential.

This type of fund is suitable for investors looking for a diversified equity investment with exposure to companies of various sizes and risk profiles.

Value Fund:

A Value Fund is a type of mutual fund that follows a value investing strategy. It primarily invests in stocks that are considered undervalued based on fundamental analysis.

The goal is to identify stocks trading at prices below their intrinsic value, offering the potential for long-term capital appreciation.

Value funds often focus on companies with strong fundamentals, stable earnings, and lower stock prices relative to their perceived intrinsic worth.

Investors in value funds typically seek a strategy that aims to capitalize on the market's tendency to sometimes undervalue certain stocks, potentially providing returns when the market corrects itself.

Sector Fund:

A Sector Fund is a type of mutual fund or exchange-traded fund (ETF) that concentrates its investments in a specific sector or industry, such as technology, healthcare, or energy.

The fund aims to capitalize on the growth potential of that particular sector. Sector funds provide investors with targeted exposure to industries they believe will outperform the broader market.

However, they also carry higher risk because their success is closely tied to the performance of a specific sector.

Sector funds are suitable for investors with a strong conviction about the prospects of a particular industry and are willing to accept the associated level of risk.

Dividend Yield Fund:

A Dividend-Yield Fund is a type of mutual fund or exchange-traded fund (ETF) that primarily invests in stocks of companies with a history of paying regular dividends.

The fund aims to provide investors with a steady income stream by focusing on dividend-paying stocks.

Dividend-yield funds typically select stocks based on the dividend yield, which is the annual dividend payment divided by the stock's price.

These funds are suitable for income-seeking investors who prioritize regular dividend income along with the potential for capital appreciation.

Hybrid Funds

Balanced Advantage Fund:

A Balanced Advantage Fund is a type of mutual fund that dynamically manages the allocation between equity and debt instruments based on market conditions.

The fund aims to provide a balance between growth and stability by adjusting its portfolio exposure to equities and bonds.

In bullish market conditions, it may increase equity allocation for potential capital appreciation, while in bearish markets, it may shift towards debt for capital preservation.

This flexibility makes Balanced Advantage Funds suitable for investors seeking a diversified and dynamically managed investment that adapts to changing market conditions.

Balanced Hybrid Fund:

A Balanced Hybrid Fund is a type of mutual fund that maintains a balanced portfolio by investing in a mix of both equities and fixed-income securities.

The goal is to provide investors with a combination of capital appreciation potential from stocks and income stability from bonds.

The fund manager actively manages the asset allocation based on market conditions and the fund's objectives.

Balanced Hybrid Funds are suitable for investors seeking a middle ground between growth and stability, offering diversification across both equity and debt instruments within a single investment.

Multi-Asset Allocation Fund:

A Multi-Asset Allocation Fund is a type of investment fund that diversifies its portfolio across different asset classes, such as stocks, bonds, and possibly other investment instruments like commodities or real estate.

The fund's objective is to provide investors with a balanced and diversified exposure to various types of assets.

Fund managers actively allocate assets based on market conditions, economic outlook, and risk considerations.

Multi-Asset Allocation Funds aim to optimize returns while managing overall portfolio risk, making them suitable for investors seeking a diversified investment strategy within a single fund.

Monthly Income Plans (MIPs):

A Monthly Income Plan (MIP) is a type of mutual fund that aims to provide regular income to investors, typically on a monthly basis.

MIPs usually invest in a mix of debt and equity instruments, with a higher allocation to debt securities. The debt component provides stability and generates regular income, while the equity component aims to enhance returns.

The objective is to distribute a part of the investment gains or income earned periodically, offering investors a steady flow of income.

MIPs are suitable for those seeking a balance between income generation and the potential for capital appreciation.

Other Funds

Flexi Cap Fund:

A Flexi Cap Fund is a type of mutual fund that has the flexibility to invest in stocks across different market capitalizations, including large-cap, mid-cap, and small-cap.

Unlike other equity funds with specific mandates, Flexi Cap Funds can dynamically adjust their portfolio allocation based on market conditions and the fund manager's outlook.

This flexibility allows them to capitalize on opportunities in various segments of the market.

Flexi Cap Funds are suitable for investors seeking a versatile equity investment with the potential for capital appreciation across companies of different sizes.

Each category serves different investment objectives and risk profiles. When building an investment portfolio, investors often diversify across multiple categories to balance risk and return. It's crucial to align your choice of mutual funds with your financial goals, risk tolerance, and investment horizon. Consulting with a financial adviser can provide personalized guidance based on your circumstances.

> Diversification is the only free lunch in investing.
>
> — Harry Markowitz

KEY PARAMETERS BEFORE INVESTING IN MUTUAL FUND

Before embarking on your journey into mutual fund investments, it's crucial to understand the key parameters that can significantly impact your financial decisions.

This guide will walk you through essential considerations, empowering you to make informed choices and navigate the complex landscape of mutual fund investments with confidence.

Equity Linked Savings Scheme (ELSS)

Now I think by now you are fully aware of the names of important funds in the market and their performance, but whenever I talk about mutual funds, I always hear one name which is ELSS so what is this ELSS?

ELSS, or Equity Linked Savings Scheme, is a type of mutual fund that helps you save on taxes while allowing you to invest in the stock market. Here's a simple breakdown:

Tax Savings: When you invest money in ELSS, you can claim a deduction on the invested amount from your taxable income under Section 80C of the Income Tax Act. This can reduce your taxable income and, consequently, your tax liability.

Equity Investment: ELSS primarily invests in stocks (equities), giving you the chance to benefit from the potential growth of the stock market.

Lock-in Period: ELSS comes with a lock-in period, which means your money is invested for a specific duration, usually three years. During this time, you cannot withdraw the invested amount.

Potential for Higher Returns: Since ELSS invests in stocks, it has the potential for higher returns compared to traditional tax-saving options like Fixed Deposits or Public Provident Funds (PPF). However, it also comes with higher market-related risks.

Choice of Dividend or Growth Option: ELSS offers investors the option to receive dividends or reinvest them for potential compounding through the dividend or growth option.

In summary, ELSS is a tax-saving investment that combines the benefits of potential equity returns with a lock-in period to qualify for tax deductions.

It's important to consider your risk tolerance and investment goals before choosing ELSS as an investment option.

Asset Under Management (AUM)

You must have heard the term AUM many times while dealing with mutual funds. Let's break down AUM or "Asset under Management" into assets and management.

Assets are things of value, like money or investments. It could be the money you have in your Piggy Bank, the value of your toys, or even the worth of your collection of trading cards.

Management means taking care of or handling something. For example, you manage your toys by keeping them organized or making sure they are in good condition.

Asset under Management (AUM) is like all the valuable things assets that someone is responsible for taking care of or managing.

This someone could be a financial advisor, a fund manager, or even you if you are handling a collection of valuable items.

Let's understand this with an example:

If you have a Piggy Bank with money in it, the total amount of money is your AUM for your "financial management".

Fund Manager: Imagine a professional who takes care of other people's money by investing it. The total value of all the money they are handling for their client is their AUM.

Investment Fund: If you and your friends pool money to invest in a collection of stocks and bonds, the total value of all those investments is the AUM of your investment fund.

Why does AUM matter? AUM is important because it shows the scale of responsibility. If someone is managing a large AUM, it means they are handling a significant amount of money, and their decisions can have a big impact.

Professionals often charge fees based on a percentage of AUM. The more assets they manage, the more they might earn in fees. For example, if they charge a 1% fee and manage ₹1,00,000 they could earn ₹1000.

AUM can also be a measure of success. If a fund manager attracts more clients or makes successful investment decisions, their AUM might grow.

So, the takeaway is that AUM is like all the valuable things assets that someone is responsible for managing. It's a way to measure this scale of responsibility, often used in finance to understand the size and success of the financial professional or investment fund.

Expense Ratio

Let's break down the expense ratio in the context of a mutual fund using a simple analogy.

Imagine our existing example of the lemonade stand. Think of starting a lemonade stand where you sell refreshing drinks. To make this happen, you need to spend money on ingredients, and cups and maybe even hire someone to help.

Running Cost: Now, running the lemonade stand comes with ongoing costs. You need to buy more ingredients, pay your helper, and maybe invest in a better stand to attract more customers.

Total Expense: The total money you spend to keep the lemonade stand up and running is like the total expenses of our mutual fund.

These expenses include everything from administrative costs, marketing, salaries of fund managers, and other operational expenses.

Total Earning from Lemonade Stand: On the other side you are making money by selling lemonade. The total revenue you generate from selling lemonade represents the total assets of the mutual fund, which is the money invested by all the investors in the fund.

Expense Ration Calculation: The expense ratio is like figuring out what percentage of your total lemonade sales (assets) is spent on running the lemonade stand (expenses). It's calculated as total expenses divided by total assets.

The formula to calculate the expense ratio is total expenses divided by total assets multiplied by 100.

$$\text{Expense Ratio} = (\text{Total Expenses} / \text{Total Assets}) * 100$$

For example, if your lemonade sales (assets) are ₹1000 and your expenses are ₹20, your expense ratio is 2% [(20 / 000) * 100].

In a mutual fund, the expense ratio represents the percentage of the fund's total assets that are used to cover the fund's operating expenses.

These expenses are deducted from the fund's returns, and the remaining amount is what investors receive.

So, the key takeaway is the expense ratio is a way to understand the cost of running a mutual fund.

A lower expense ratio is generally considered better for investors because it means more of the returns go to them rather than covering high operational costs.

When comparing mutual funds, it's common for investors to consider expense ratio as a part of their decision-making process.

A medium to higher 'Expense Ratio' value is considered better.

Compound Annual Growth Rate (CAGR)

CAGR is another very common and important factor in analyzing the mutual fund.

Imagine a tree growing. Think of investing in a mutual fund like planting a tree. You put some money (seed) into the mutual fund, and you expect it to grow over time.

As years go by, the tree grows taller and branches out. Similarly, the value of investment in the mutual fund grows over time due to the returns generated by the fund's investment.

Now understand how CAGR works:

CAGR is like looking at the average annual growth of your tree over a specific period. It considers how much the tree has grown each year, compounding the growth.

Suppose you planted a tree with a certain initial height and after several years it has reached a certain final height.

CAGR is calculated by figuring out the consistent annual growth rate that would lead to the same overall growth from the initial height to the final height.

CAGR can be calculated by analyzing any fund through its 3 Years and 5 years history.

Growth over 3 years:

After three years, your investment tree has grown taller. The height it has reached after this period represents the value of your investment at the end of the 3 years.

Calculating 3-year CAGR:

A 3-year CAGR is like figuring out the average annual growth rate that, when applied over the 3 years, would lead to the same overall growth from the initial investment to the value after 3 years.

The formula to calculate a 3-year CAGR is:

$$\text{3-Year-CAGR} = \left(\frac{\text{Ending Value}}{\text{Beginning Value}} \right)^{(1/3)} - 1$$

where 3 is the number of years

Growth over 5 years:

Now let's Fast forward to five years. Your investment tree has continued to grow and its height at the end of 5 years represents the value of your investment over this long period.

Calculating 5 years CAGR:

5 5-year CAGR is calculated similarly, determining the average annual growth rate that, when compounded over 5 years would lead to the same overall growth.

The formula to calculate a 5-year CAGR is:

$$\text{5-Year-CAGR} = \left(\frac{\text{Ending Value}}{\text{Beginning Value}} \right)^{(1/5)} - 1$$

where 5 is number of years

In the mutual fund context, the CAGR values provide a way to understand the average annual growth rate of the fund over the respective 3-year and 5-year periods. It's a useful metric for investors to assess the fund's performance over different time frames.

So, the key takeaway is the 3-year and 5-year CAGR to help investors gauge the average annual growth rates of their investments in a mutual fund over a specific period.

These metrics consider the compounding effect, providing a more comprehensive view of the fund's performance.

> A higher 'CAGR' value is considered better.

Sharpe Ratio

The Sharpe ratio is a measure that helps investors understand the return of an investment compared to its risk. Economist William F. Sharpe developed it.

It looks at the difference between the return of an investment and the risk-free rate of return (like the interest of a safe government bond), considering the level of risk taken.

The formula for the Sharpe ratio is (Return of investments − Risk-Free rate) / Standard Deviation of the investment.

$$\text{Sharpe Ratio} = \frac{(\text{Expected Return Portfolio} - \text{Risk-Free Rate})}{\text{Standard Deviation Portfolio}}$$

Let's say you have two investments. Investment A has an average return of 10% and Investment B has an average return of 15%. If the risk-free rate is 3%, the Sharpe ratio helps you to see which investment gives you more return for the risk taken.

For Investment A: (10% - 3%) / Standard Deviation

For Investment B: (15% - 3%) / Standard Deviation

A higher Sharpe ratio indicates that an investment is giving you more return for the risk you are taking. It's a way to compare investments on a risk-adjusted basis.

Investors often use the sharper ratio to make decisions about which investments to include in their portfolios. Or higher Sharpe ratio suggests a more efficient use of risk to achieve returns.

It's important to note that the Sharpe ratio is just one tool among many to evaluate investments. It assumes that higher returns are prettier and that investors prefer a higher return for a given level of risk.

While the sharper ratio is widely used, it does have limitations. For instance, it assumes that the distribution of returns is normal, which may not always be the case in real financial markets.

So, the takeaway is that the Sharpe ratio is a useful metric for investors to access the risk-adjusted performance of an investment.

It helps answer the question: "Is the return I'm getting from this investment worth the level of risk I'm taking?" A higher Sharpe ratio generally suggests a more attractive risk-return profile.

A medium to higher 'Sharpe Ratio' value is considered better.

3-Year Annual Rolling Return

The 3-year annual rolling return is a way to measure how well an investment, like a mutual fund, has performed over different three-year periods.

Instead of looking at just the total return over one fixed three-year span, the rolling return considers many overlapping three-year periods.

For example, if you're looking at a mutual fund's 3-year rolling return in 2023, it would calculate the average annual return from 2020 to 2023, then shift the window to calculate the average annual return from 2021 to 2024, and so on.

This provides a more dynamic and continuous view of the fund's performance, helping investors see how it has fared during various market conditions.

In simple terms, it's like looking at a series of three-year snapshots throughout the fund's history to get a better understanding of its consistency and performance over time.

A higher '3 Year Annual Rolling Return' value is considered better.

Summary

After exploring the key parameters to select the best mutual fund, it's evident that a thoughtful approach is essential for making informed investment decisions.

By considering factors such as AUM, CAGR, Expense Ratio, Sharpe Ratio, 3-year Annual Rolling Return, etc., investors can craft a well-rounded strategy that aligns with their financial goals.

Diversification remains a cornerstone, spreading investments across various asset classes to mitigate risk.

Regularly reviewing and reassessing the chosen funds ensures that the portfolio stays aligned with evolving market conditions and personal objectives.

Ultimately, the journey of selecting the best mutual fund is dynamic, requiring ongoing attention and adaptability.

Armed with knowledge and a strategic mindset, investors can navigate the intricate landscape of mutual funds, unlocking the potential for long-term financial growth and stability.

> Mutual Fund is a basket of stocks. It allows you to buy ownership in a bunch of different companies without having to buy the shares yourself.
>
> - John Bogle

WHICH MUTUAL FUND IS CORRECT FOR ME?

Now we understand what is Mutual fund but now the question is what are the types of Mutual Funds and how do you choose them?

2023 has started in a very different way, especially when it comes to the stock market. Many people in the market are scared because they have seen the first downturn.

So obviously, many people don't understand how to see their money. They have started to invest in the FDs. But here we will see why mutual funds are better than FD's.

I also want to tell you why long-term investing in the stock market is a great idea which you hopefully know but you are not sure of what to do about it.

The best way to enter the stock market is not by picking up stocks that you think will make you rich overnight. instead, to be very disciplined about investing in the portfolios of stocks.

Here we will try to answer some common questions. #1, if you want to start investing in equity at any age then what percentage of your monthly income should go towards equity, and what should go into safer assets?

#2, what role do mutual funds play in equity? Why are they important? Why are they better than picking up stocks? #3, how to select a mutual fund?

If you want to start your equity investing journey and you are tired of doing FDs, or you are afraid of FDs, then what should be the split?

There is a very good rule which is called the 100 - X rule. It says that if your age is X then 100 - X, which is 75, should be in percentage terms as much as you invest in equities and the rest should be in safer assets which could be fixed-income assets.

To be more precise if you are of X age, then X percentage of your monthly investment should go into fixed income or safe assets and then 100 - X percent should go into the equities. This is all long-term.

Now the important part of this chapter is how to select a mutual fund. I won't tell you which mutual fund you have to select because that becomes trickier, but I'll tell you which type of mutual fund you must select.

There are fundamentally three types of mutual funds. First, the mutual fund we call a debt mutual fund.

What is a debt mutual fund? As soon as you have an FD, it is a debt mutual fund. This mutual fund will invest in those assets where we get a fixed rate of return.

These are largely corporate bonds and government bonds. FDs can also be there. Anything that guarantees a fixed rate of return.

So, the benefit is if you invest in this mutual fund, then you will get a very straight fixed rate of return. It is never equal or exact to FD, but it runs in a very tight range.

Second, I call it an equity or growth mutual fund. These are mutual funds that invest in equities or the stock market.

So, there is no fixed income or fixed rate of return. And the third combination, which is a combination of these two is usually called a hybrid or balanced mutual fund.

These mutual funds are the combination of some fixed incomes and equities or stock markets, and the ratio of that is determined by your risk appetite.

So, if you are 25 years old and you want a mutual fund that invests 25% in debt or a fixed rate of return and 75% in equities then a mutual fund is the best suit for it.

But there is a lot of confusion in this, especially in equities. When I say investing in equity, then who should I invest in? Should I invest in Reliance, or should I invest in Tata? Should I invest in a random fertilizer company or any chemical company that is launched by a company that is growing at a very fast rate of stock price? Should I invest in Pharma, or should I invest in Banking, or should I invest in telecom? So, these are the thoughts when we are thinking of buying a stock.

To answer all the above questions, I have a simple model that you can use to find out your risk appetite for investing.

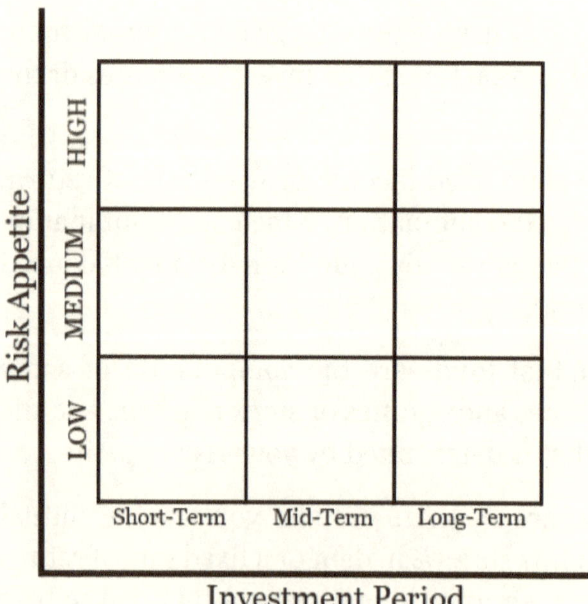

Imagine that there are 9 squares, three are equal to X-axis and three are equal to Y axis.

On the X axis, define how long you want to invest. Is it short-term? In my definition, a short term is less than 2 years. Is it a midterm? which is between two to five years. Or a long-term which is greater than five years.

These are three usual investment horizons. And then you need to ask yourself how much risk you are willing to take. Low risk, medium risk, or higher risk. Now when I say high risk doesn't mean that you say no to it. It means that you will take a little high risk, but it will be necessary because it may serve a higher return over a long period.

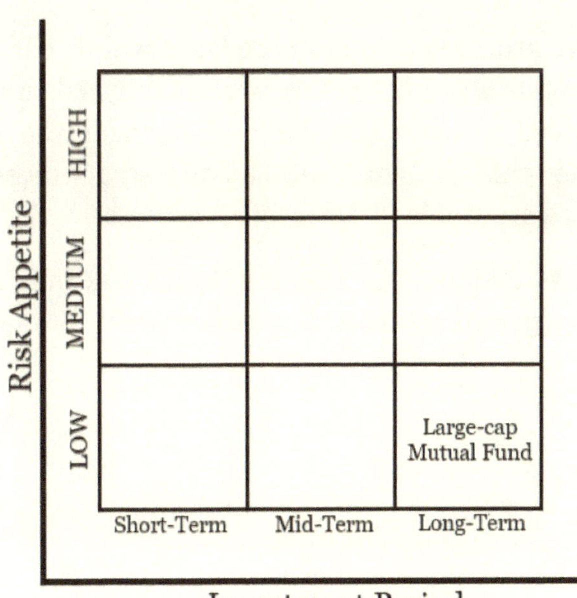

So now seeing the above table, there are nine different types of approaches depending on where you are.

So, what do you do? If you want to invest for more than five years, the question you ask yourself is where should I invest for more than five years?

The low-risk category investment is called large-cap mutual funds. That means mutual funds that are only invested in equity and only those companies are investing which are large-sized.

For example, Reliance, Tata, Infosys, Wipro, Asian paints, HDFC, ICICI, etc.

Why is this low risk? The lower risk is because these companies are very proven in terms of their track record.

They have grown very well in the last several years. The corporate structure is very well established, and management is stable. And the fund manager who is managing this is going to ensure that these companies are stable in terms of all aspects.

So, you are taking a considerably lower risk over a long-term period by investing in large-cap mutual funds.

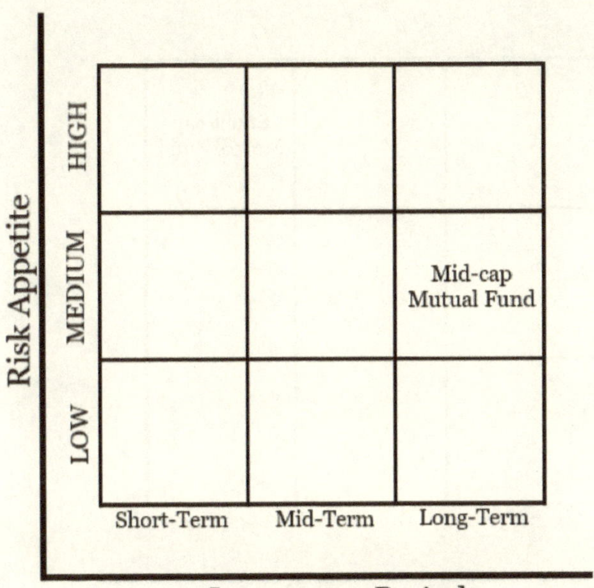

So now what happened in medium-risk long-term mid-cap mutual funds? These are the companies whose market capitalization or the size of the company is somewhere in the middle.

This has grown from small but not big yet. Why is there more risk in this? Because any company may get closed, or any company may grow slowly, or any company gets distressed.

All these parameters will affect the mutual fund. But it is possible that the deep decline could be harder. However, over a long period, this is proven to give higher returns.

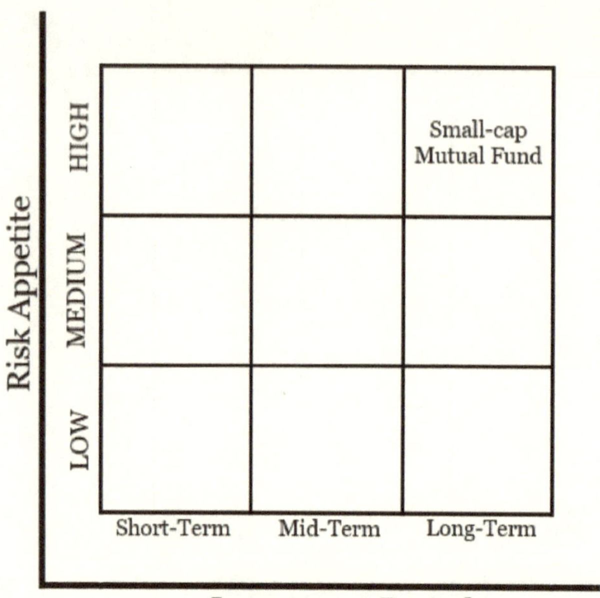

Now if you want to take high risk for the long term then where to invest? And there is something called small-cap mutual funds.

These are the companies that are very small right now. You are investing in equities and because these are very small, anything can happen to them.

So that's why it is very high risk. But because of high risk, you can earn higher returns.

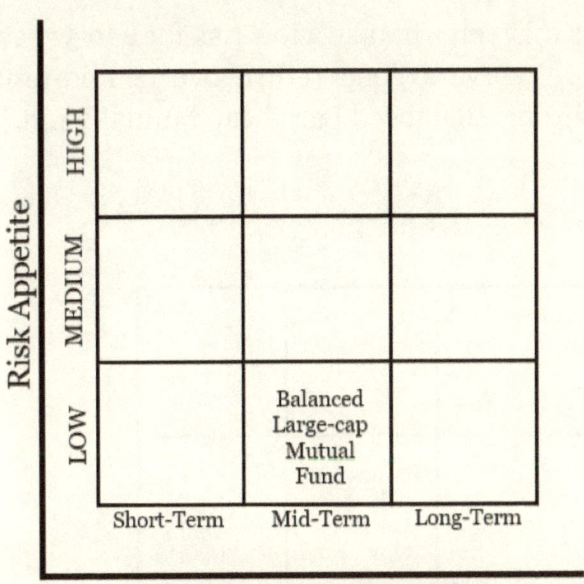

Let's look at the midterm. In the mid-term, you have to invest your money for 2 to 5 years and you should look for a mutual fund that covers low risk, medium risk, and high risk.

In low risk, you can select something called the "Balanced Large cap" mutual fund. This means a mutual fund will invest in fixed income or equities, but equities will only invest in large capital companies.

So, you are getting this stability of equities because it's low risk and you are also getting fixed income which is a combination.

It means that you will take a low risk for 2 to 5 years and it will serve a good return over a mid-term period through Balanced Large-cap Mutual Fund.

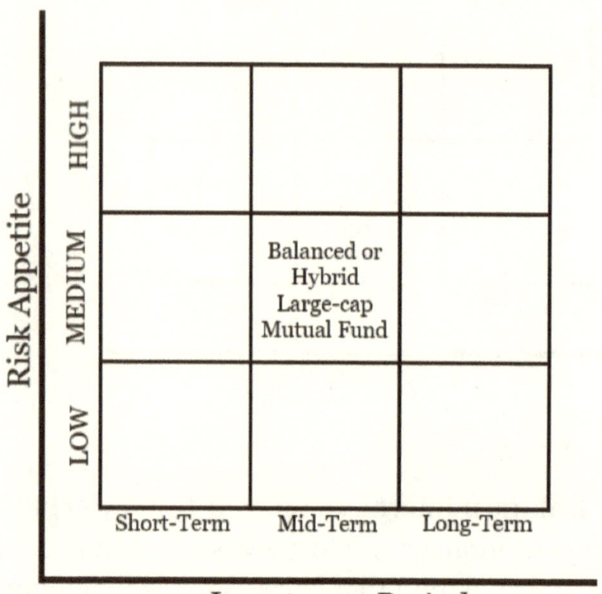

For medium risk, it is like a hybrid large cap or a balanced large cap. Both are the same.

The period for medium risk is also defined as 2 to 5 years. You can select a Balanced Large-cap mutual fund that will invest in fixed income/equities of large-cap companies or a Hybrid Large-cap Mutual fund that invests in a blend of more than one asset class.

These could be debt/fixed deposit types of securities, equity, or commodities (Gold).

Mostly hybrid funds invest in debt and equity in various proportions. Balanced funds are just one type of Hybrid funds.

Usually, the investments for medium and low risk are the same.

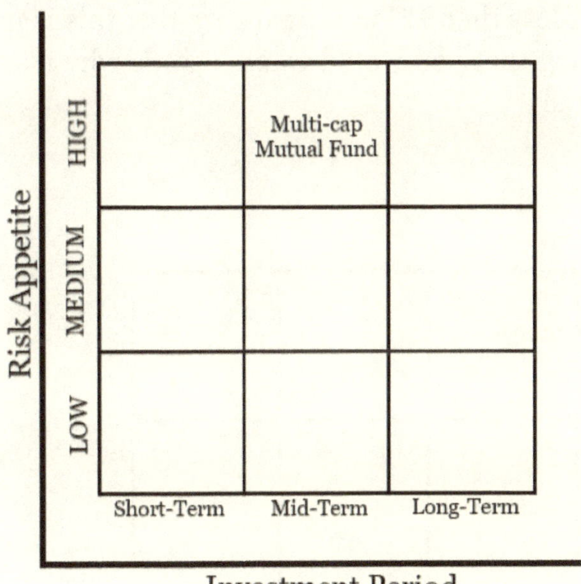

Now, if you want to go for high-risk in the mid-term period of 2 to 5 years then go for multi-cap mutual funds.

Multi-cap funds are the ones that invest in equities but across all types of companies i.e., large, medium, and small companies. That's why it's at high risk because the full investment is in equities.

As there is no fixed income, there is a possibility that the invested amount would not grow in 2 to 5 years. And as per the history, it's happened many times that the equity market hasn't performed.

So, in those 2 to 5 years, you may invest in these equities and your money won't move at all. It is also possible that you will get a return of 0, 1, 2, or 4% which is less than FD and I am sure that this is not something that you would want. That is why it's at higher risk.

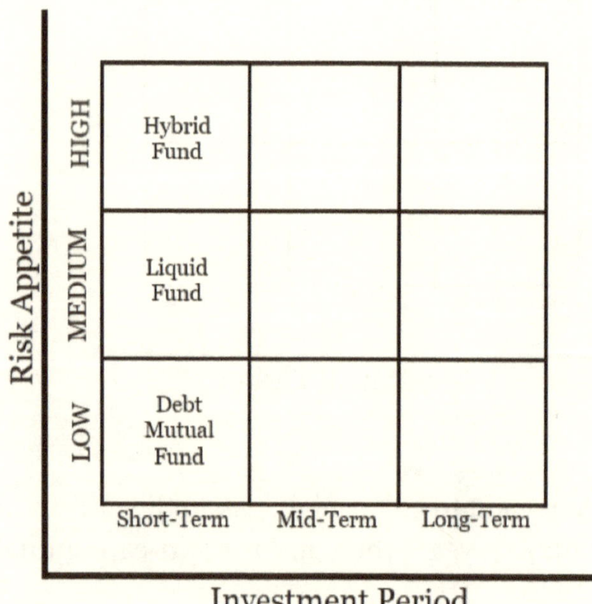

Finally, what is a short-term Investment? If you want to invest in the short term, which is less than 2 years, then ideally you shouldn't invest in equities.

Because in two years, equities may not perform as you expect, and you should not play with your money. That is not a wise investment.

So, if you want to invest below 2 years, it should be mostly in Liquid or Fixed income mutual funds. What are these mutual funds?

As I mentioned, these are the mutual funds that invest in a fixed rate of return whether it's Government Bonds, Corporate Bonds, FDs, etc., and that is why they ensure a stable return over a while.

You will park your money here only and only because you are investing for a short period. So, for short-term low-risk, the best option is a debt mutual fund.

For short-term, medium risk, the option will be liquid funds. And for short-term high-risk means, you are ready to take high risk in the short term which is a hybrid fund that will have a lot of debt, but some percentage of equity can be there because you are willing to take that high risk.

So, this is the total graph and that is how you would go about picking your mutual funds.

Now the question is what is my risk? Ideally, this is completely driven by one's risk appetite. But if you would ask my recommendation that if you are spending ₹100 then do you pull all that money in low risk? Or put the whole high risk, the answer is 'No', you should follow a combination approach.

My suggestion is 70% of ₹100 i.e., ₹70 should invest in low risk, 25% in medium risk, and 5% in higher risk.

That means if you are investing for the long term, which is greater than five years, then put 70% of that money in large-cap mutual funds, 25% of that mutual fund in mid-cap mutual funds, and then 5% of that money in small-cap mutual funds.

Similarly, for any other time horizon, this will tell you the nice happy mix where you will get a good return and you will not take more risks for the time.

> With a Mutual Fund, you can sleep soundly knowing you are not putting all your eggs in one basket. It's like having a team of expert pilots navigating your financial voyage.

BULL AND BEAR MARKET

Now, we are going to understand the concept of bull market and bear market. It's very simple and straightforward. I'm sure you must have seen these terms in the news and on social media.

So, you might know a little bit, but let's just say that you don't know anything, and let's understand. It's really simple, bull market and bear market are just two different ways of saying how the stock market is performing in a country over a sustained period.

A bull market is when the stock market is doing well, and share prices are continuously going up Bear market is the opposite situation where share prices are continuously falling over a sustained period.

It's not like today if the share price has gone up then immediately you cannot say that it's a bull market situation, it's not like that.

It has to be over a sustained period like a few weeks, months, or years. If the stock market index is going up during a particular time or sustained time, specifically more than 20% from recent lows then it is referred to as the Bull market.

The complete opposite situation is the Bear market. If the stock market index is going down during a particular time, specifically more than 20% from recent highs, it is referred to as the Bear market.

These are opposite situations, now let's understand the characteristics of the bull and bear market. The characteristics of the bull market are Strong demand and weak supply. What does that mean?

It means that many Investors in the stock market are ready to buy the securities by the shares. but there are very few investors who are ready to sell their shares.

This situation is called strong demand and weak supply many people want to buy but there are very few people who want to sell. So, because of this, the prices will go higher, and it is called strong demand and weak supply.

Another point here is high investor confidence. What does that mean? High investor confidence means the investors are thinking very highly of the stock market.

They are ready to put their money into the stock market. It is because they are seeing that the prices are shooting up and they expect that prices are going to go even higher, and they will be making huge profits by selling it later.

Due to this, there will be more inflow in the stock market. Many people will invest. This will lead to a robust economic environment. There is very little unemployment, and companies are making big profits.

And then the other thing is sufficient disposable income will remain with the people. So, what is disposable income? Disposable income is the income that is Left after paying their expenses and taxes and everything so if they have sufficient Disposable income then they will spend it.

Maybe people will spend it on luxurious goods, etc. So, if they spend a lot then, of course, the companies will be making profits, so it's all connected, and then inflation will also be less.

This scenario is called a robust economic environment. Overall, the economy is doing well, the GDP is doing good, and everything is good. So, that's a bull market characteristic.

Now let us talk about the Bear Market. A bear market is exactly the opposite.

There will be weak demand and high supply, prices will continuously fall, and the entire market sentiment will be negative, if the sentiments are negative then, of course, everyone will be willing to sell the shares and get out of the market.

In short, when people know that the sentiment in the market is negative (weak demand and high supply) everyone will try to sell and ultimately it results in high supply because no one wants to buy, and no one wants to invest, which is called weak demand.

This scenario leads to low investor confidence because everyone is scared.

There is a pessimistic situation in the stock market and low investor confidence. No one wants to put their money into the stock market and make a loss because everyone is thinking that the prices will fall and if I invest now, I will make a loss.

This kind of situation is called low investor confidence and a poor economic environment.

If there is a recession, it's called a poor economic environment i.e., low GDP and high inflation. Now the question that comes to your mind is, how the high inflation will affect the market? Let me tell you, that high inflation leads to high unemployment and insufficient disposable income. These are the reasons for the poor economic environment and the characteristics of a bear market.

Now after all this discussion, I'm sure you must be wondering why are we using the name of these two animals, bull and bear, why not cat and dogs?

It's very simple, if you just check the way these animals attack then you will understand. To attack, the bull swipes up with its horns and the bear swipes down with its paws. Prices are increasing, which means the market swipes up, and when the prices are falling means, it swipes down.

Let's understand this with an example, imagine the stock market is like a roller coaster. Sometimes, it goes up a lot, and that's called a "bull market."

One of these times was from 2009 to 2020, even though there was a tough period called the Great Recession. Then, the COVID-19 pandemic hit, and everything stopped, like hitting the emergency brakes on the roller coaster.

After that, the government did a bunch of things to help the economy, like giving it a boost. This made the stock market go up again—another bull market.

This happy ride lasted until December 2021 when things started slowing down. The people in charge said they would make it a bit harder for the economy to grow by increasing interest rates (imagine making the roller coaster track a bit steeper).

Because of this news, people got worried, and the stock market turned into a "bear market," which means it started going down.

This happened in 2022 when the interest rates went up like they said they would. So, it's like the roller coaster went from going up a lot to going down because the people in charge made some changes.

While each bull market may be driven by different factors, they tend to have similar traits:

Big Price Growth: Bull markets happen when prices of things like stocks keep going up a lot for a while. It's like a race where the winner keeps setting new records.

Happy Investors: When the market is doing well, people who invest money feel good. They get excited and might even try riskier investments. This excitement helps prices go up even more.

More Jobs: During bull markets, there are usually fewer people without jobs. More people working means more money to spend, which helps companies make more profit.

Growing Economy: Bull markets often happen when the whole economy is doing well. Things like businesses growing, more people getting jobs, and positive signs in how the economy is doing all play a part. Sometimes, a bull market starts even before the economy has fully recovered from a tough time.

Now, investing is a common strategy. It's like buying something, maybe a stock (which is like a share in a company), and holding onto it for some time, hoping its price will go up.

The idea is that if you believe the thing, you bought will become more valuable, it's like holding onto your special toy because you expect it to become more popular.

In happy times for the stock market (bull markets), many investors feel confident that prices will keep going up.

So, they like the idea of buying something and holding onto it (the buy and hold approach) because they're optimistic that what they own will become even more valuable in the future.

It's a bit like keeping your favorite toy because you believe lots of people will want it, and its value will go up.

So, in simple terms, a bull market is like a happy time for the economy and investments, where

everything is going up, people are working, and
everyone is feeling good about it.

	Bull Market	Bear Market
Performance	Asset prices rising to new highs consistently	Asset prices are down 20% from recent high
Economic Indicators	Expanding GDP, Rising investor confidence, declining unemployment	Shrinking GDP, falling investor confidence, Rising unemployment
Average Lifetime	5.3 years (since 1943)	12 months (since 1646)
Frequency	6.1 years (since 1943)	5.8 years (since 1946)
Average Return	169.5% (for bull markets between 1943-21)	-33.6% (for bear markets between 1945-21)

Source: Yardeni Research

There are other concepts that we always use while
dealing with mutual funds, the first one is a
lumpsum investment.

LUMPSUM INVESTMENT

Lump sum investment in mutual funds refers to investing a large amount of money in a mutual fund scheme all at once, in a single transaction.

It is the opposite of systematic investment, where investors regularly invest smaller amounts at regular intervals.

Here is a simple explanation:

Imagine you have a sum of money, let's say a big bag of coins. Instead of putting a few coins into your investment every month, with a lumpsum investment, you decide to invest the entire bag of coins all at once in the mutual fund.

Let's understand the key points about lumpsum investment:

One-time investment: It is a single, substantial investment made at a specific point in time.

Timing and Market Conditions: Since you are investing a lumpsum, your returns are influenced by the market conditions at the time of investment. If the market is going well, you benefit; If not, your investment could be affected.

Suitable for Windfalls: Lumpsum investments are often made with a significant amount of money, from a bonus, inheritance, or the sale of an asset.

Volatility Consideration: Due to the potential impact of market volatility, lumpsum investments can be riskier in the short term. The value of the investment may fluctuate more compared to a gradual investment approach.

Long-term Perspective: Lumpsum investments are often considered with a long-term perspective. Over an extended period, the impact of short-term market fluctuations may be balanced out, and the investment may have the opportunity to grow.

Diversification: Even with a lumpsum investment, it's essential to consider diversification. Diversifying the investment across different asset classes or mutual fund schemes can help manage risk.

Professional Advice: Given the potential risks associated with lumpsum investments, some investors seek professional financial advice before making such a significant commitment.

Financial advisors can provide insights into market conditions, investment strategies, and potential risks.

Periodic Review: Investors who make lumpsum investments should periodically review their portfolio and financial goals. Regular assessments can help ensure that the investment strategy aligns with evolving financial objectives.

Remember, the choice between lumpsum and systematic investment depends on individual preferences, risk tolerance, market conditions, and financial goals.

Both approaches have their merits, and the decision should align with the investor's unique circumstances and investment strategy. If uncertain about market timing, some investors prefer strategies like systematic transfer plans to gradually move money from safer investments to mutual funds over time.

Benefits of lump sum investment

Let's quickly understand the concept. The first advantage is convenience. Suppose you have a monthly SIP of 10,000 rupees scheduled for the 10th of each month.

Now, imagine you receive a performance bonus on the 15th. Are you going to wait until the next 10th to invest it? No. With lump sum investing, you have the convenience to invest the entire bonus all at once, without being tied to a specific date.

The second advantage is timing the market. If you possess enough knowledge about the market and can identify support levels, you might decide to invest a substantial amount when you believe the market is at its lowest and is likely to bounce back.

A prime example is someone who invested a significant sum in March 2020 when the market was at its lowest. I'm sure that person would be quite happy with their decision today.

This is precisely what we mean by lump sum investing at a lower point.

Let's break down when to opt for lump sum investments. Firstly, if you're not a salaried individual but, let's say, a businessperson who receives a substantial sum after completing a project, like in the film industry where you get a big chunk of money after finishing a movie, lump sum investment might be a better option for you.

Secondly, even if you are a salaried person and you receive a performance bonus, that could be another opportunity for a lump sum investment.

Now, considering the duration for which you should keep your money invested, whether through SIP or lump sum, the ideal period remains the same: at least 5 years.

However, a crucial difference lies in when each investment pattern works best.

SIP generally proves effective in a falling market, allowing you to benefit from lower average costs as you invest consistently during market downturns.

On the other hand, lump sum investing typically works well in a rising market, where you can capitalize on the upward trend to potentially maximize returns.

SYSTEMATIC INVESTMENT PLAN (SIP)

Now let's start by understanding what an SIP is. Well, I could have chosen the path of telling you the definition of SIP and then explaining it to you about it.

But I think let's put it in a very simple format. I'm sure many times it happens that parents give some kind of pocket money to their children.

The child then chooses to save a part of their pocket money and chooses to put that or save that in a piggy bank.

Eventually over months as he saves more and more, the piggy bank will be full, and once it is full you will ideally take that entire money and put it in a bank.

So, what did that child do, was it an SIP? I would not say that it is a systematic investment plan as such.

Instead, I can say that was a systematic saving plan of saving every single month, and the entire amount from that piggy bank was put in the bank in one shot, let us say in an FD, that was a lump sum investment.

I will give you another example. I am sure you might have seen that many times the bread earner of the family gives some part of his income to the homemaker and many times she prefers to keep or save some money in some kind of box.

So, what does the homemaker do? Every single month she'll set aside some money that her husband is giving her.

She saves that amount with her or in some container and then when it comes to a specific decent enough amount, she'll go and put it in the bank.

That small amount that she was keeping aside monthly was again an example of systematic saving, not systematic investment, and the lump sum amount that she put in the bank, let's say FD is a lump sum investment.

But understand the drawbacks in both cases. The money isn't increasing either in the piggy bank or in the container where she's storing it, correct? So, what could have been a more effective way?

A better way could be putting that amount, say 100 or 500 rupees every month, in a recurring deposit. Might that have been a straightforward description of a systematic investment plan?

Yes, because this process will happen systematically over a specific period. The same thought process if I apply for a mutual fund, wherein I invest some money, say 500 rupees, every month in a mutual fund scheme that is referred to as a SIP in a mutual fund.

Let's understand the benefits of a SIP.

Rupee cost averaging

Rupee cost averaging in mutual funds is like having a smart savings plan for your investments.

Imagine you decide to invest a fixed amount of money, let's say Rs. 1,000, in a mutual fund every month. Some months, the mutual fund's price might be higher, and you'll get fewer units for your Rs. 1,000. In other months, when the price is lower, you'll get more units.

Now, here's the cool part: because you're investing the same amount regularly, you end up buying more units when the price is low and fewer units when the price is high.

Over time, this helps average out the cost of your investment. It's like being a savvy shopper – you buy more when prices are low and less when they're high.

Rupee cost averaging reduces the impact of market ups and downs because you're consistently investing. It's a way to smooth out the bumps in the market road, and in the long run, it can be a smart strategy for building wealth.

Disciplined investing

Disciplined investing in mutual funds is a bit like sticking to a savings routine for your investments. Let me break it down:

Imagine you decide to set aside a fixed amount of money regularly, let's say every month. This could be Rs. 1,000 or any amount you're comfortable with. Now, you make a commitment to yourself that, come what may, every month, you'll invest that fixed amount in a mutual fund.

Here's the key – you stick to this routine, regardless of whether the market is up, down, or sideways. It's like having a financial plan and following it diligently.

Disciplined investing helps you avoid getting swayed by short-term market fluctuations. If the market is doing well, great! You continue with your routine. If it's not doing so well, that's okay too – you're still investing.

This consistency over time can have a positive impact. When prices are low, your fixed amount buys more units, and when prices are high, it buys fewer. It's a way of averaging out the cost of your investment.

Flexibility

If something doesn't go as planned, let's say, for instance, due to an unexpected event like the COVID-19 pandemic. Imagine you've been regularly investing Rs. 2000 every month through SIP, but unfortunately, due to a salary cut caused by the pandemic, you can't afford to invest that much anymore.

Can you temporarily pause your SIP for a while? Yes. Can you even stop it for an extended period? Absolutely. So, flexibility is all about having the freedom to adjust your investment plan when faced with unexpected situations.

Flexibility in mutual funds is like having a financial superhero cape that allows you to adjust your plans when life throws curveballs.

For example, you regularly investing a fixed amount, say Rs. 5,000, every month in a mutual fund.

Now, life isn't always predictable. There might be times when unexpected things happen – maybe you have to tighten your budget, or there's a sudden expense.

Flexibility in mutual funds means you have the power to adapt. If you need to pause or reduce your monthly investment for a while because of a financial hiccup, you can do that.

You're not locked into a rigid plan. It's like having the freedom to tweak your investment strategy to match your current situation.

Maybe you had to cut back on your investment for a few months, but once things stabilize, you can pick up where you left off. It's about having control and making your investments work for you, even when life takes unexpected turns.

So, flexibility in mutual funds is your financial superhero's ability to adjust, adapt, and continue your investment journey with confidence.

> Think of a Mutual Fund as a rocket ship for your wealth, propelling you towards your financial goals at a speed you couldn't achieve alone.

When to choose SIP?

Let's break down when to consider choosing an SIP and how to determine if it's suitable for you. First off, if you have a steady income source, like a salary, it's highly beneficial.

Knowing a fixed amount will be credited to your bank account regularly allows you to save and invest a portion of it every month.

Secondly, for those earning in the range of 10,000, 15,000, or 20,000, who often feel like they can't make significant investments due to their lower income, SIP is a great solution.

Starting small and gradually increasing your investment over time can lead to substantial gains.

Thirdly, SIP performs exceptionally well in a declining market. Imagine investing at 100, then at 90, and continuing as the market goes down.

Your average cost becomes lower because you're consistently investing at lower levels, making SIP effective even when the market is falling.

Fourthly, the ideal time to start an SIP is as soon as possible. In Sanskrit, there's a saying, "Shubhasya Sighram," which means it's auspicious to start things quickly.

So, rather than delaying and waiting for a special occasion or a new resolution, starting your SIP as early as possible is key for long-term success.

Remember, the longer you wait, the more potential growth you might miss out on.

A common question I receive is whether one can engage in SIP for just one year. Specifically, when considering SIP in an equity mutual fund, a one-year timeframe is quite short.

In my opinion, an ideal time frame for SIP in such funds would be five years or more. This longer duration allows for a more realistic and potentially fruitful investment, considering the typical fluctuations and trends in the equity market.

Mutual funds are like tiny seeds that can grow into mighty trees, with the magic of compounding interest working its wonders.

Lumpsum Vs. SIP

Let's debunk the myth of SIP versus lump sum and analyze when lump sum might be better.

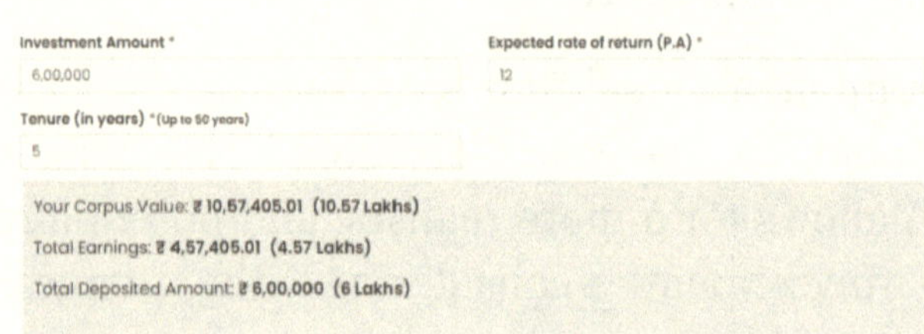

Suppose I decide to invest a lump sum of 6 lakh rupees at a 12 percent average return rate in an index fund for a period of five years.

The future value of this lump sum investment would be 10.57 lakh rupees.

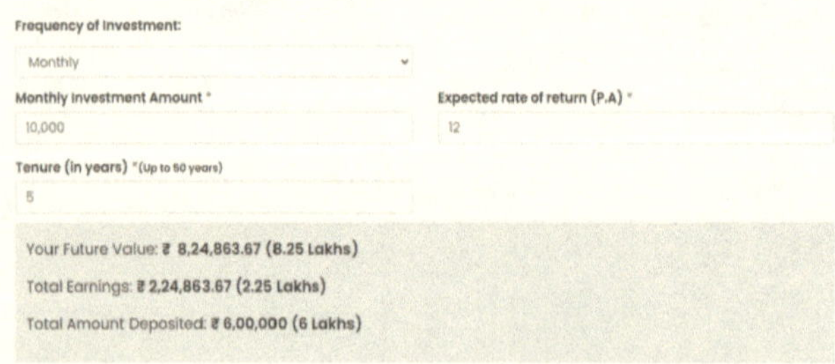

Now, consider an alternative scenario where I invest 10,000 rupees every month for the same five-year period, resulting in a total investment of 6 lakh rupees. Assuming the same 12 percent average return, the future value of this SIP investment would be 8,24,864 rupees.

So, when we compare the two, the lump sum investment yields a higher future value of 10.57 lakh rupees, while the SIP investment reaches 8,24,864 rupees.

The reason for this difference is straightforward. In lump sum, I invested 6 lakh rupees all at once, and this amount compounded over the entire five years.

In contrast, in an SIP, the initial investment in the first month was only 10,000 rupees, and the last investment in the fifth year, from 10,000 to 20,000 rupees, was invested for just one month.

This variance in the timing of investments explains the difference in the future values between lump sum and SIP.

Think of a mutual fund as a team of expert investors working tirelessly to grow your wealth, even while you sleep.

SYSTEMATIC TRANSFER PLAN (STP)

Let's simplify the concept of a Systematic Transfer Plan (STP). Imagine you have some money, and you want to invest it in the stock market, but you're worried about putting it all in at once because the market can go up and down. A Systematic Transfer Plan (STP) is a smart way to handle this.

Here's how it works:

Start in a Safe Place: You first put your money into a safe and stable investment, like a debt fund. This is like a temporary parking spot for your money.

Transfer Gradually: Instead of putting all your money into the stock market at once, you transfer a fixed amount regularly from the safe place (debt fund) to the stock market (equity fund). This can be weekly, monthly, or at any regular interval you choose.

Capture Market Opportunities: Because you're transferring money regularly, you take advantage of both low and high points in the stock market.

If the market is down one week, you buy more units at a lower price. If it's up the next week, you buy fewer units but at a higher price.

In simple terms, STP is a steady and strategic way to move your money from a safe place to the stock market over time, helping you manage the ups and downs of the market.

Let us understand with an example to illustrate how a Systematic Transfer Plan (STP) works:

Suppose you have a lump sum amount of Rs. 1,00,000 that you want to invest in the stock market, but you're concerned about market volatility. You decide to use STP to manage this.

Start with a Debt Fund: You choose a debt fund, which is considered a safer and more stable investment. You invest the entire Rs. 1,00,000 in the debt fund.

Scheduled Transfers to Equity Fund: Now, you set up an STP to transfer a fixed amount regularly from the debt fund to an equity fund. Let's say you decide to transfer Rs. 5,000 every month. STP is scheduled monthly.

Market Participation: In the first month, your Rs. 5,000 is transferred from the debt fund to the equity fund, buying units of the equity fund at the current market rate.

If the market is up, you buy fewer units with Rs. 5,000. If it's down, you buy more units at a lower price.

Continuous Process: This process repeats every month. So, over the next several months, you continue transferring Rs. 5,000 from the debt fund to the equity fund.

Advantages:

If the market is doing well, you benefit from having some money in the equity fund and participating in the gains.

If the market is down, you also benefit because you're buying more units at lower prices.

Let's assume the market fluctuates over the year:

Month 1: The equity market is up, so you buy fewer units.

Month 2: The market is down, so you buy more units. And so on...

Over a year, you've not only participated in the stock market but also managed your risk by spreading your investment over time.

This gradual approach is designed to capture both the highs and lows of the market, potentially optimizing your overall returns.

SYSTEMATIC WITHDRAWAL PLAN (SWP)

Systematic Withdrawal Plan (SWP) is a feature in mutual funds where investors can regularly withdraw a predetermined amount from their investments. It provides a steady income stream, allows for flexibility in withdrawal amounts and frequencies, and keeps the remaining investment in the fund, participating in market movements. SWP is often used by retirees or those seeking periodic payouts from their investments.

The primary purpose of SWP is to provide investors with a regular and predictable stream of income from their mutual fund investments. This can be especially useful for retirees or individuals looking to supplement their income.

How SWP Works:

Initial Investment:

You start by investing a lump sum amount in a mutual fund.

Choosing Withdrawal Amount and Frequency:

You decide how much money you want to withdraw regularly (withdrawal amount) and how often (withdrawal frequency). This could be monthly, quarterly, or annually.

Setting Up SWP:

You fill out the necessary paperwork with the mutual fund company to set up the SWP. This includes specifying the withdrawal amount, frequency, and other details.

Market Conditions:

Regardless of market conditions, the mutual fund will sell units equivalent to the specified withdrawal amount and credit the proceeds to your bank account. This process continues based on the chosen frequency.

Remaining Investment:

After each withdrawal, the remaining investment stays within the mutual fund, allowing it to continue participating in market movements.

Example Scenario:

Let's say you have invested Rs. 10,00,000 in a mutual fund. You decide to set up an SWP of Rs. 5,000 every month.

At the start of the first month, the mutual fund sells units equivalent to Rs. 5,000 and credits that amount to your bank account.

The remaining investment in the mutual fund continues to be subject to market fluctuations.

The process repeats every month, providing you with a steady income.

Advantages of SWP:

Regular Income: SWP offers a systematic and regular source of income, making it useful for individuals needing periodic payouts.

Market Participation: Your remaining investment continues to participate in market movements, potentially allowing for capital appreciation.

Flexibility: You have the flexibility to adjust the withdrawal amount, and frequency, or even stop the SWP as per your financial needs.

Considerations:

It's crucial to monitor the performance of your investment, as sustained poor market conditions can impact the long-term sustainability of the SWP.

Keep an eye on the taxation aspects, as withdrawals may have tax implications depending on the nature of the mutual fund and the holding period.

Keep in mind that the success of a SWP depends on the performance of your investment. If the market performs well, your investment may grow, and you can continue withdrawing. If the market faces challenges, it may impact the long-term sustainability of your SWP. It is a way to turn your mutual fund investment into a regular income stream, allowing you to enjoy the benefits of your investment while still participating in the market.

In summary, SWP is a financial strategy that allows investors to create a consistent income stream from their mutual fund investments while retaining the potential for market-related growth in the remaining investment.

ANALYZE MUTUAL FUND RETURNS BEFORE BUY!

If you're feeling a bit puzzled about the various returns in mutual funds, worry not! In this section, we're going to break down three types of returns: Annual return, Trailing return, and Rolling return.

Annual Return

The Mutual Fund Annual Return is the percentage increase or decrease in the value of your investment in a mutual fund over one year. It's a measure of how well your investment has performed during that year.

Example:

Let's say you invested Rs. 10,000 in a mutual fund on January 1st, and a year later, on December 31st, the value of your investment has grown to Rs. 11,000.

Calculation:

Initial Investment: Rs. 10,000

Final Value: Rs. 11,000

Mutual Fund Annual Return Formula:

$$\text{Annual Return} = \left(\frac{\text{Final Value} - \text{Initial Investment}}{\text{Initial Investment}} \right) * 100$$

Using this formula:

$$\text{Annual Return} = \left(\frac{11{,}000 - 10{,}000}{10{,}000} \right) * 100 = 10\%$$

So, in this example, the Mutual Fund Annual Return is 10%. It means your investment grew by 10% over the one year.

Understanding the annual return helps investors assess the performance of their mutual fund investments and compare them with other investment options. Keep in mind that past performance doesn't guarantee future results, but it provides insights into how the fund has historically performed.

Key Takeaways:

The annual return provides a snapshot of the fund's performance on a yearly basis.

Investors use this information to make informed decisions about their investment strategy.

It's important to consider the risk associated with the investment along with the return for a comprehensive analysis.

Understanding and tracking the Mutual Fund's Annual Return is crucial for investors to make informed decisions and assess the overall performance of their investment over time.

Trailing Return

Trailing return is a way to measure how well a mutual fund has performed over a specific period leading up to the present day. It's like looking back over the fund's shoulder to see its historical performance.

Time Frame: Trailing return considers the performance of a mutual fund over a specific trailing period, leading up to the current date. The trailing period is measured backward from the present.

Continuous Measurement: It provides a continuous measure of how the fund has performed over time. As time progresses, the trailing return updates, considering the changing value of the investment.

Historical Performance: Trailing return reflects historical performance. It helps investors understand how the mutual fund has fared over the chosen trailing period.

Comparative Analysis: Investors often use trailing returns to compare the performance of different funds or to assess how a fund has performed relative to a benchmark or category average.

Example Scenario:

We have seen in the previous example that the 1st year return was Rs. 11,000.

Let's extend the example: Suppose, in the second year, the current value of the investment is Rs. 14,000.

Trailing Return Calculation for the Second Year:

$$\text{Trailing Return (Second Year)} = \left(\frac{14{,}000 - 10{,}000}{10{,}000} \right) * 100 = 40\%$$

So, the Mutual Fund Trailing return for the second year is 40%.

Key Takeaways:

Trailing return is a dynamic measure that updates as time progresses.

It provides a historical perspective on a fund's performance.

Investors use it for ongoing evaluation and comparison of mutual funds.

Mutual Fund Trailing Return is a valuable tool for investors to assess how well a fund has performed over a chosen period, leading up to the present day. It aids in making informed investment decisions and understanding the fund's historical performance dynamics.

Rolling Return

Rolling return is a way to assess a mutual fund's historical performance over various consecutive and non-overlapping periods.

Instead of looking at fixed time frames like a year, a rolling return allows us to see how the fund has performed in multiple, continuous periods.

Example:

Suppose you have a mutual fund, and you want to calculate the rolling return over one year. If today is December 31st, 2023, you would calculate the return for the one year ending on each previous day for the past, say, three years.

Investment Start Date: January 1st, 2021.

Investment End Date (rolling period 1): December 31st, 2021.

Rolling Return Calculation for Period 1:

$$\text{Rolling Return (Period 1)} = \left(\frac{\text{Value on December 31st, 2021 - Initial Investment}}{\text{Initial Investment}} \right) * 100$$

Now, you repeat this calculation for each subsequent one-year period, shifting the end date backward:

Investment End Date (rolling period 2): December 31st, 2022.

Investment End Date (rolling period 3): December 31st, 2023.

You would calculate the rolling return for each of these periods to get a comprehensive view of how the fund has performed over various one-year intervals.

Key Points:

Dynamic Evaluation: Rolling return allows for a dynamic evaluation of a fund's performance over multiple rolling periods, providing a more comprehensive picture.

Continuous Analysis: It helps investors continuously analyze the fund's historical performance without being confined to fixed time frames.

Comparison:

Investors often use rolling returns to compare how a fund has performed relative to benchmarks or other funds over different time intervals.

Rolling return is a versatile tool for investors to assess a mutual fund's performance over various time frames, helping them make more informed decisions based on a broader historical context.

RISKS INCLUDED IN MUTUAL FUNDS

When you hear advertisements for Mutual Funds, there's usually a rapid disclaimer stating, "MutualFundInvestmentsAreSubjectToMarketRrisks,ReadAllSchemeRelatedDocumentsCarefully."

In simpler terms, it's a quick reminder that when you invest in Mutual Funds, your money is influenced by how the market performs, and there's a possibility of both gains and losses.

To make informed decisions, it's crucial to thoroughly read and understand all the documents related to the investment schemes.

So, let's dive a bit deeper into each of these mutual fund risks:

Market Risk

The overall stock or bond market can fluctuate. When it goes up, your investment grows; when it goes down, your investment can decline.

Example: If the stock market rises, the value of your equity mutual fund may increase. Conversely, if it falls, your investment may decrease.

Risk of Loss:

Investments always come with the chance of losing money. The value of your investment can be influenced by various factors like market conditions, economic events, or the poor performance of the companies the mutual fund has invested in.

Example: If the companies in which your mutual fund is invested face financial troubles, the fund's value may decline, leading to potential losses for investors.

Credit Risk:

If a mutual fund invests in bonds, there's a risk that the issuer of the bonds (like a company or government) may not be able to repay the borrowed money.

Example: If a company defaults on its bonds, the value of the bond holdings in the mutual fund may be impacted.

Liquidity Risk:

Liquidity refers to how easily an investment can be bought or sold. Some investments may be less liquid, meaning it could take longer to sell them without affecting their price.

Example: If a mutual fund holds investments in less-traded securities, selling them quickly might be challenging, especially during market downturns.

Interest Rate Risk:

Changes in interest rates can affect the value of certain investments, particularly bonds. When interest rates rise, bond prices tend to fall.

Example: If a mutual fund holds a significant amount of bonds, an increase in interest rates could lead to a decline in the value of those bonds.

Inflation Risk:

Inflation erodes the purchasing power of money over time. If your investment returns are lower than the inflation rate, your real returns may be negative.

Example: If your mutual fund doesn't outpace inflation, the actual value of your money may decrease in terms of what it can buy.

Diversification Risk:

Not spreading your investments across different types of assets exposes you to higher risk because poor performance in one area can significantly impact your entire investment.

Example: If all your money is invested in technology stocks and the tech industry experiences a downturn, your overall investment could suffer.

Management Risk:

The success of a mutual fund is influenced by the decisions made by the fund manager. Poor investment choices or strategies can impact the fund's performance.

Example: If the fund manager consistently makes suboptimal investment decisions, it can lead to underperformance compared to the market or similar funds.

Understanding these risks is crucial for investors. While risks are inherent in investing, they can be managed by diversifying your portfolio, staying informed, and aligning your investments with your financial goals and risk tolerance. It's advisable to consult with a financial advisor to make well-informed investment decisions.

TAXES ON MUTUAL FUNDS

In this section, we will discuss how income tax is relevant specifically to mutual funds and what types of taxes are associated with them. It aims to explain the taxation aspects related to mutual funds.

In simpler terms, when we talk about taxes on mutual funds, it means that when you make a profit or incur a loss from your mutual fund investments, you might have to pay taxes.

There are two main types of taxes for mutual funds: capital gains tax, which is applicable when you sell your mutual fund and make a profit, and dividend tax, which is related to the earnings distributed by the mutual fund.

In this chapter, we will discuss how these taxes apply to these two types of gains. Additionally, this chapter will cover the basics of mutual funds, and it's important to note that there are three main types of mutual funds.

Understanding the three types of funds is important because the tax rates applicable to mutual funds, as per the income tax regulations, vary based on these categories.

We also will discuss the current taxation that is applicable from 1st April 2023.

Investment of more than 65% in Equity

Let's start with the first part. How is the overall taxation? Taxation has been divided into three parts. The first part is *equity-based allocation.*

This type involves mutual funds like Axis Mutual Fund or ICICI Mutual Fund etc. that primarily invest in stocks.

The tax implications, including rates and calculations, are linked to the equity market. It can cover small-cap, mid-cap, and large-cap stocks, depending on the fund's strategy.

Equity Allocation	> 65%
STCG	15% without indexation
LTCG	10% after 1 year holding period (No tax till Rs.1L capital gain

Applicable to Fund Category	- All domestic equity funds - Equity Saving Funds - Arbitrage Funds - Aggressive hybrid Funds
Taxation may vary based on the Fund manager	- Dynamic asset allocation funds - Multi-asset funds - Balanced Advantage funds

In simpler terms, when we talk about equity funds, it means that more than 65% of the money in these funds is invested in stocks during a financial year, starting from April 1st, 2023. Now, let's understand the tax implications for these funds.

If you invest in such funds and sell them within a year, you'll be subject to a short-term capital gain (STCG) tax, which is 15% of the gains.

On the other hand, if you hold onto these funds for more than a year before selling, you'll be liable for a long-term capital gain (LTCG) tax, which is 10% of the gains. Additionally, there's a benefit where if your capital gain is up to 1 lakh, you won't be taxed, but any gain exceeding 1 lakh will be subject to the 10% tax rate.

This rule remains the same as before in the context of equity funds with over 65% allocation in stocks; there hasn't been any change in this section.

Now, let's shift our focus to the second section, which is recently introduced.

We have a new section in play. If the equity allocation in a fund ranges from 35% to 65%, which often characterizes hybrid funds, it falls into this category.

The minimum threshold for equity investment is 35%, and the maximum is 65%. The tax calculation is based on the average equity allocation over the past year.

Equity Allocation	35 - 65%
STCG	Marginal Tax Rate
LTCG	20% with indexation after 3 year holding period
Applicable to Fund Category	Balanced hybrid funds
Taxation may vary based on the Fund manager	- Dynamic asset allocation funds - Multi-asset funds - Balanced Advantage funds

Let's understand more about how this taxation works:

Holding Period Less Than 3 Years:

If you keep your money in this type of fund for less than 3 years, the tax will be calculated based on your marginal tax rate. This means you'll pay the tax rate corresponding to your tax bracket.

For instance, if you fall into the 30% tax bracket and gain 10,000 rupees, you'd pay 3,000 rupees in taxes.

Holding Period More Than 3 Years:

If you hold onto your investment for more than 3 years, you'll face a long-term capital gains tax, which is a flat 20%. However, you'll also benefit from indexation.

Indexation considers inflation, and it works like this: Let's say you earned an 8% return in 3 years, and inflation was 6%.

The government provides a CII index for this. So, you subtract the inflation rate from your return, resulting in a 2% taxable gain. Applying the 20% tax rate to this 2% gain, you get the tax liability.

To sum it up, this new section applies to funds with equity allocations ranging from 35% to 65%.

The taxation varies based on the holding period – less than 3 years incur tax at your marginal rate, while more than 3 years incur a flat 20% tax with the benefit of indexation.

Previously, this type of taxation was referred to as debt taxation. However, now it applies specifically when the equity allocation in a fund falls within the range of 35% to 65%.

So, the rules and considerations we discussed are now applicable only to funds within this specific equity allocation range.

Now, if the fund has less than 35% equity allocation, which is typical for all debt funds and some other hybrid funds, the taxation process simplifies. In this case, you'll be taxed only on the gains you've made.

For example, if you invested 1 lakh rupees and gained 10,000 rupees, you'll pay tax based on your applicable tax bracket.

The holding period doesn't affect this scenario; whether you hold the investment for 1 year, 2 years, 5 years, or 10 years, the tax will be applicable when you redeem the investment, starting from that financial year.

Equity Allocation	0 - 35%
STCG	Marginal Tax Rate
LTCG	Marginal Tax Rate
Applicable to Fund Category	- All debt funds - All FoF - Gold ETF - International FoF - Conservative hybrid funds
Taxation may vary based on the Fund manager	- Dynamic asset allocation funds - Multi-asset funds - Balanced Advantage funds

So, in summary, the tax implications for mutual funds depend on whether it's an equity fund, a debt fund, or a hybrid fund that combines both.

Each type has its own tax rules, and understanding these distinctions is crucial for investors.

INDEXATION AND ITS IMPACT

In this section, we will understand about the Indexation and its Impact on Tax Liability. We'll explore what indexation is, how it works to reduce your tax liability, and the financial instruments where you can benefit from indexation.

What is Indexation?

Indexation is a mechanism designed to account for the impact of inflation on your investments. As we know, inflation gradually erodes the purchasing power of money over time. Indexation allows investors to adjust the purchase price of an asset by considering the effect of inflation.

How Does Indexation Work?

Let's illustrate with an example:

Suppose you invested 50,000 rupees in a debt mutual fund scheme in June 2016 and redeemed it for 80,000 rupees in June 2022, making a profit of 30,000 rupees. Since the holding period exceeds 36 months, the long-term capital gain tax rule applies, and indexation is available.

If we calculate the long-term capital gain without considering inflation, then the tax that needs to be paid is Rs 6000/-.

Capital Gain = Rs. 80000 − Rs. 50000

= Rs. 30000

Total Applicable Tax = Capital Gain * 20%

= Rs. 30000 * 20%

= Rs. 6000

Now let's calculate it by applying indexation.

To calculate the taxable profit, you adjust the purchase price (50,000 rupees) for inflation. This adjustment is done using the Cost Inflation Index (CCI) table available on the Income Tax website.

Financial Year	Cost Inflation Index
2016 − 17	264
2017 − 18	272
2018 − 19	280
2019 − 20	289

2020 − 21	301
2021 − 22	317
2022 - 23	331

CCI in FY17 (the year of investment): 264

CCI in FY23 (the year of redemption): 331

$$\text{The Inflation Adjusted Purchase Cost} = \left(\frac{\text{Original Cost of Acquisition}}{\text{CCI of FY17}} \right) * \text{CCI of FY23}$$

$$= \left(\frac{50000}{264} \right) * 331$$

$$= 62689$$

Now, you divide the original cost of acquisition (50,000 rupees) by the CCI of FY17 and multiply it by the CCI of FY23. The inflation-adjusted purchase cost is 62,689 rupees.

Instead of the apparent profit of 30,000 rupees, the adjusted capital gain considering indexation is 17,331 rupees.

With a long-term capital gain tax rate of 20%, the effective tax liability is 3,462 rupees, which is 2,558 rupees lower than it would be without indexation.

Capital Gain after Indexation   =   Rs. 80000 - Rs. 62689

                                =   Rs. 17331

Total Applicable Tax   =   Rs. 17331 * 20%

                                =   Rs. 3462

Important Considerations:

Indexation is applicable only for long-term capital gains, where an asset is held for more than 36 months.

Indexation benefits do not apply to equity shares or equity mutual funds.

Indexation benefits can be availed for other capital gains, such as the sale of a house, jewelry, debt funds, etc.

In essence, indexation is a valuable tool for investors to account for the impact of inflation on their returns, reducing the tax burden on capital gains.

AVOID THESE COMMON MISTAKES

Considering Mutual Funds with low NAVs for investment

The first mistake is associating mutual fund investment with low NAVs. Unlike stocks, where buying early can mean more potential profits, mutual funds work differently.

In mutual funds, you're not investing in a single company's growth potential but in a mix of stocks that can change based on market conditions and the fund manager's decisions. Your returns depend on the difference between the investment and redemption NAVs, not the initial NAV level.

New mutual funds or New Fund Offers (NFOs) might have lower NAVs, but they lack a proven track record. It's wiser to consider established mutual funds with a history of success, as they provide more confidence in your investment decision.

Investing lower amounts

Another common mistake is investing in small amounts. For example, some people start SIPs with 1000 rupees each month in one mutual fund and another 1000 rupees in a different one.

This could be because you're testing the waters of the stock market with a modest investment. However, the mistake occurs when, despite experiencing good returns, you don't increase your contribution.

By not increasing your investment, the majority of your money remains in low-yield options, affecting your overall returns.

If you find that the investment is going well and feels safe, don't hesitate to increase your contributions in line with your financial goals. Taking that step can lead to better returns in the long run.

Investing a lumpsum amount in ELSS in the last quarter of the year.

Another common mistake is making a lump sum investment in ELSS (Equity Linked Savings Scheme) in the last quarter of the year. Data indicates that approximately 50% of ELSS investments occur in the final quarter of the year, with around 20 to 25% taking place in March, the last month of the financial year.

By opting for a lump sum investment, you miss out on the rupee cost-averaging benefit provided by SIP (Systematic Investment Plan). SIP allows you to achieve an average purchase price by investing systematically throughout the year, as detailed in our video on the benefits of SIP.

There's also a risk associated with market timing. What if the market is at an all-time high when you make this lump sum ELSS investment? Just for the sake of saving taxes, you might end up investing in an overvalued market. It's advisable to avoid this mistake and consider systematic investment, even for your tax-saving requirements.

Investing lumpsum in Equity when Market PE is above 25.

Another common mistake is making a lump sum investment in equity when the market's PE (Price-to-Earnings) ratio is above 25.

The PE ratio of major indices like Sensex and Nifty provides an overall indication of the market's valuation. It helps you understand whether the market is overvalued.

Investing a lump sum when the market is overvalued can lead to minimal returns or even losses. Specifically, if the Nifty PE is above 25, it's recommended to consider an alternative strategy.

Instead of directly investing in equity, allocate your lump sum to liquid funds and then execute an STP (Systematic Transfer Plan) to gradually move funds into equity funds. This approach can potentially mitigate risks associated with an overvalued market.

Not investing for the right duration

Another common mistake is not aligning your investment duration with the right type of mutual fund.

Many people hesitate to invest in the stock market due to fear, often stemming from a lack of knowledge. However, understanding which investment vehicle suits specific time horizons can boost confidence.

For short-term investments up to 3 years, debt funds are a suitable choice. Balanced funds are appropriate for a 3 to 5-year horizon, while large-cap funds are recommended for 5 to 7 years. If you're looking at a 7 to 10-year timeframe, multi-cap funds are a good option. For periods exceeding 10 years, consider small and mid-cap funds.

When it comes to ELSS (Equity Linked Savings Scheme), don't limit yourself to the mandatory 3-year lock-in period. Instead, stay invested for 5 to 7 years, given that ELSS falls under the category of equity funds.

Mismatching your investment duration with the appropriate fund type can lead to losses and potentially form incorrect opinions about mutual funds. Therefore, choose a fund aligned with the right duration, and you're likely to experience favorable returns.

Investing based on last year's performance of a fund.

Another common mistake is investing based on last year's performance. When aligning your financial goal with the right type of mutual fund, consider looking at historical data relevant to your investment horizon.

For instance, if you're considering mid-cap funds suitable for a 10-plus-year investment, analyze the historical performance of various funds over the past decade. Choose a fund that has demonstrated consistency over this period.

For liquid funds, ideal for a 3-month investment duration, prioritize funds from reputable fund houses with lower expense ratios.

Applying logic to historical data is crucial in making informed investment decisions. It's important to note that outstanding performance in the previous year may not necessarily make a fund the best choice if it lacks consistency.

Over diversification

Another common mistake is over-diversification. We often receive emails containing an extensive list of selected funds, seeking our opinion on the choices.

Optimal diversification would typically involve a maximum of two funds per financial goal. Over-diversifying can complicate the analysis of your returns, making it challenging to assess and manage your investment portfolio effectively.

Not Matching your risk profile with the kind of fund within a category.

Another mistake to avoid is failing to align your risk profile with the type of fund within a category. Various mutual fund categories consist of funds with different risk profiles, such as conservative, aggressive, and growth-oriented funds.

For instance, in the ELSS category, the Franklin India Tax Shield Fund is more suitable for conservative investors, the Access Long-Term Equity Fund caters to growth-oriented investors, the Aditya Birla Sunlife Tax Relief 96 Fund is suitable for aggressive investors, while the IDFC Tax Advantage Fund is more suitable for very aggressive investors.

Imagine you're not an aggressive investor, but due to specific circumstances, you had to opt for an aggressive category like mid-cap funds to meet your financial goal.

In this case, it's crucial to select a fund within that category that aligns with your risk profile.

Buying Dividend option when not required.

Another common mistake is opting for a dividend option when it's not necessary. During your working years, you likely have a steady source of income, making dividends an additional income stream you might not depend on.

People often choose this option, thinking it could supplement their primary income. However, relying on dividends can hinder the compounding effect of your investments.

In reality, the declared dividend amounts are minimal, offering little impact as an additional income source.

For instance, the declared dividend could be as low as 0.6 rupees per unit annually. While this might seem negligible, it still affects the compounding effect, impacting your financial goals and returns.

It's essential to consider whether the dividend option aligns with your overall investment strategy and financial objectives.

Common Mutual Fund Abbreviations:

NAV: Net Asset Value

AMC: Asset Management Company

AUM: Assets Under Management

MF: Mutual Fund

SIP: Systematic Investment Plan

SWP: Systematic Withdrawal Plan

STP: Systematic Transfer Plan

ELSS: Equity Linked Savings Scheme

ROE: Return on Equity

ROI: Return on Investment

NAVPS: Net Asset Value Per Share

CAGR: Compound Annual Growth Rate

L&T: Load and Trail (referring to mutual fund expenses)

FMP: Fixed Maturity Plan

KYC: Know Your Customer

AMFI: Association of Mutual Funds in India

SEBI: Securities and Exchange Board of India

CDSL: Central Depository Services Limited

ISIN: International Securities Identification Number